# CONFEDERATE STREETS

# Confederate Streets
## ERIN E. TOCKNELL

2011 • Benu Press, Hopkins MN

Copyright © 2011 by Erin E. Tocknell

All rights reserved. No part of this book may be reproduced in any form or by any means, electronic or mechanical, including printing, photocopying, recording, or by any information storage or retrieval system, without permission in writing from the publisher.

10 11 12 13   7 6 5 4 3 2 1   FIRST EDITION
Paperback edition and electronic edition
Printed in the United States

Design by Claudia Carlson, www.claudiagraphics.com
Text set in Jensen and display in Transit
Map of Nashville, Ten. © 2010 Google, Map data © 2010 Google

ISBN 10: 0-9844629-0-2   ISBN 13: 978-0-9844629-0-2   Paperback
ISBN 10: 0-9844629-1-0   ISBN 13: 978-0-9844629-1-9   Hardcover
ISBN 10: 0-9844629-2-9   ISBN 13: 978-0-9844629-2-6   E-Pub

LIBRARY OF CONGRESS CONTROL NUMBER: 2010935258

PUBLISHER'S CATALOGING-IN-PUBLICATION DATA

Tocknell, Erin E.
  Confederate Streets / Erin E. Tocknell.
  p. cm.
  ISBN 978-0-9844629-1-9 (Hardcover)
  ISBN 978-0-9844629-0-2 (Pbk.)
  ISBN 978-0-9844629-2-6 (E-pub.)
  Includes bibliographical references.
  1. Tocknell, Erin E. 2. Racism --Southern States --History --20th century --Anecdotes. 3. Southern States --Race relations. 4. Nashville (Tenn.)--Biography. 5. Nashville (Tenn.)--Race relations. 6. Southern States --Social life and customs --20th century --Anecdotes. I. Title.

E185.98.T63 2011
323.1/196073—dc22         2010935258

P.O. Box 5330
Hopkins, Minnesota
55343-9998
www.benupress.com

*For Mom, Dad, and Cathleen*

"We are made of where we've come from, molded by landscape, weather, harbors, hunger, and war, as much as by individual ancestors. The experience of the place—its struggles, strife, and horrors—accrues, even if we haven't personally experienced it. We are, still, its inevitable consequence."
—Dr. Deborah Tall, *A Family of Strangers*

"I am leaving, I am leaving." / But the fighter still remains.
—Paul Simon and Art Garfunkel, "The Boxer"

# Contents

| | |
|---|---|
| Visits | 3 |
| Confederate Streets | 7 |
| What Trees Become | 26 |
| That's What We're Doing Here | 36 |
| Our Most Segregated Hour | 50 |
| Learning Glory | 65 |
| DeFord's Blues | 73 |
| 17th and Jo Johnston | 89 |
| Leave the Driving to Us | 106 |
| Rowing Through the Ruins | 123 |
| | |
| *Acknowledgments* | 135 |
| *Partial Bibliography* | 139 |
| *About the Author* | 141 |

# CONFEDERATE STREETS

# VISITS

Our lives are comprised of stories, but they generally do not unfold the way we tell them, tidy and separate, like the photos accordioned in a father's wallet. Instead they are printed haphazardly, smudged with fingerprints, their edges crooked and uncut, some pieces dropped on the floor and lost. The stories we *tell* have conflicts, climaxes, and dénouements. The stories we *live* reel forward and through themselves until the endings become beginnings of their own—and beginnings are endings as well. Last summer, as I was researching and writing these essays, I witnessed three such endings-and-beginnings.

I spent Memorial Day weekend in New York City, meeting the new fiancée of a friend from grade school. Five days later, I sat with two other longtime friends in the Civic Center in Huntington, West Virginia, and watched their son graduate from high school. Four days after Chris's graduation, I was in a maternity suite at Baptist Hospital in Nashville, holding the newborn daughter of two other friends. The chair was stiff and the baby, wrapped like a burrito in her hospital blanket, felt soft and heavy against the crook of my elbow. I was last in a long line of visitors that day. The new parents looked at me and baby Jenny with heavy-lidded eyes. After a few minutes I awkwardly transferred Jenny to her father's arms, said goodbye, and left the room.

In the hallway, I passed the Neo-Natal Intensive Care Unit and parents dressed in scrubs waiting to be allowed in to the ward. I rode the elevator two floors with a woman whose stoic face was betrayed by streaked mascara. When the doors slid open, a delivery man checked his invoice, sighed, and wheeled a cart full of flower baskets into the space I had deserted. I walked out through the Emergency entrance, turned the key in the ignition of my Subaru, and drove up to a red light. Facing the skyline, I waited for the light to turn green.

The skyscrapers were monolithic hulks of concrete and steel, their windows flaring orange in the dusk. Usually, this is a sight so familiar I don't give it any thought. But as the sunset reflected in the glass that evening, I realized that each window opened into an office. Each office belonged to someone who sat at a desk for about eight hours everyday; each desk was likely decorated with photos of weddings and graduations and babies. The roll of film tucked in my camera had friends smiling in Central Park, a family standing around their son in his graduation robe, a new daughter asleep in her father's arms. Three sets of stories. In the skyline, thousands more. In the world, thousands of skylines. This is what Jenny was coming into—a world of hospital bracelets pressed into scrapbooks, save-the-date cards, and square cardboard hats. A world where mascara streaks over foundation, where a basket of flowers sits beside a pitcher of water that sits beside an IV pole, where sealed doors open and shut, and neighbors take casseroles to houses. A world of little pink hats and plastic tubing, dress shoes and elastic booties, one-hour film developing, sterile gloves, lace, Kleenex bunched in fists, and diplomas tied with ribbon.

The traffic light changed, and all those stories felt heavy and immutable in the June air. I'd planned to meet a group of friends at a restaurant, but suddenly I couldn't stand the idea of being around anybody. I needed to sit alone somewhere, to sort through all those moments and file them like cards in an old library catalogue. But where could I go? My parents' yard—where, as I teenager, I'd sit at the crest of the hillside and watch darkness gather around the pine trees—would have been my first choice. In June, the grass is fragrant, the air above it dotted with lightning bugs, but it is not my parents' yard anymore. An artist and her sister had purchased it, and the house, the previous winter. With night coming on, the city parks didn't seem like a good option. I ended up shutting off the car in the parking lot of my old church and sitting in the grass beneath a hackberry tree. The sanctuary was behind me. When I lay back, I could see its steeple and two yellow stars in the hazy city sky above it.

I stayed there, staring at the sky with my hands clasped beneath my head as the events of the past 10 days flickered past like a filmstrip. Austin and Ann, a board game, glasses of bourbon. Their wedding would be at a resort in the Catskills in January. Lynn and I on the porch in Huntington, watching Chris walk to his car, Eddie carrying the green robe on a hanger—Chris would leave for college that August. Jenny barely the length of her father's forearm, one hand wrapped around Kris's knuckle; Allison propped on pillows, watching. I played the scenes over and over until they were mostly played out and I had room in my mind for other things. I sat up. The stories arranged and filed themselves. The world beyond the grass, the steeple, and its two stars returned.

Although it hadn't occurred to me as I was driving, the church itself was as responsible for my state of mind as the friends who'd brought it on. As a child at Calvary United Methodist, I'd gone to Sunday School, children's choir, and youth group with Kris and Allison. All the while, Austin was going to school with me, and we knew each other's church friends. In seventh grade, Lynn and Eddie were youth group counselors and Chris hung around begging for games of catch. My friends and I have walked the pathways beneath the trees on Christmas Eves and Easters and innumerable Sundays in between. We posed by the forsythia bush for Confirmation photos, used the parking lot as a staging area for ski trips, retreats, and service projects. Much of the foundation of my life, and its stories, took root around the spot where I'd stretched across the grass and cleared my head.

If we are willing to look, place connects us with the people who help us bear our lives, but it also links us to lives we never consider, lives that have intertwined with our own and created shared yet distinct histories. We press toward our next new beginning and use a shallow lens to examine these stories. But they deserve closer investigation. Last June, even as I was in the midst of writing about the past, it took me some time to recognize the role of place and history as events unfolded in my friends' lives. All we are today is marked by the landscape, its history, and the people we share it with, whether we've held their babies or not. The fact that we rarely consider this doesn't make it any less true.

That night, while I sat in the churchyard, cars passed through the parking lot toward the back of the church. Our collective memories are so short, I worried someone might accuse me of trespassing. However, the SUVs and sedans kept moving. Perhaps their drivers hadn't noticed the dark figure beneath the hackberry. Probably they also hadn't noticed the stone "slave wall" that once denoted a plantation boundary and now separates Calvary from Hillsboro Road, or the Confederate battle trench near the church's back door, as they rushed inside for their meetings.

I watched the steeple that night and felt the weight ease out of the air around me. Again, I heard the steady drone of traffic on Hillsboro Road, and it sounded like cars rather than a thousand untold stories rushing past my ears. I could stand up, feel my head clear, and be happy. I thought about catching up with my friends for dessert or some drinks.

---

I wrote these essays on visits. I slept in guest rooms, drove along lengths of the Cumberland River that I hadn't known before, jogged through neighborhoods I'd always known about but never really experienced. With the chapter of my life where Nashville is "home" so solidly behind me, I found a cleaner divide between the present and the past. I could hold it out like a globe, examine pieces of history from all angles, think about place and memory and photographs and street names—hold them to the light. In many ways, Nashville is the city I expected to find—charming and friendly, but marked by deep divisions along lines of race and class. Marked so deeply and completely that the lines themselves often seem to have disappeared into the landscape. I was surprised myself at how easy it was to cross the boundaries which had always seemed integral to my mental map of the city. The windows were no longer catching light on the horizon. I was actually stepping through them.

These essays are about the stuff we don't really notice—roads, churches, photographs, school buses, front yards, radio broadcasts, sports, morning papers, swimming pools, classrooms, choir rehearsals, live music. They are about the invisible pieces of life—my own, but they touch on many stories. The meaning of our lives must be there in the everyday world, lived out by both strangers and friends in the spaces we inhabit. These essays record what I've seen, what I've come to understand, and why I think it matters.

I hope this reads as praise, not for a perfect world, but for ours.

# CONFEDERATE STREETS

### GRAPE VINES AND DREAM SUMMERS, 1984

Young Southerners, especially privileged white ones, learn their history slowly. Race is rarely discussed, so it hangs in the air like a mist. Many in my generation who grew up in Southern cities can remember the moment when they became aware of segregation, and the subsequent moments through the decades when they realized that the old social order was not completely dead and was, in fact, shaping their lives. My city began to reveal these truths to me when I was in first grade. But in the summer of 1984, the places I loved still seemed whole and beautiful.

In conversation, my parents refer to it as "the dream summer." They say this without sentimentality. It is fact that those months were everything a summer should be. My little sister, Cathleen, was just over a year old. She took tottering walks around our yard and played in the sandbox my father had built for her. Cathleen was obedient, and round. I was less obedient, leaner, and about to begin first grade. I wore blue sneakers with silhouettes of kangaroos on the tongues and, inspired by their bounding image, leapt everywhere. I refused ponytails. My hair streamed behind me like the mane of a palomino.

For most of June, I packed a swimsuit, towel, bag lunch, and blue jeans into a tan duffel bag with a cross and oak leaf printed on the side, then waited on a cinderblock wall at the top of my driveway for the car pool to the Oak Hill Day Camp. At Oak Hill, I learned to ride horses and sang camp songs like "Sippin' Cider" and "A Boy and a Girl in a Little Canoe."

Green dominates the landscape of my memories in southwestern Nashville. We lived in a log house halfway up a ridge in a neighborhood called Forest Hills, bordered by Green Hills to the north, Oak Hill to the east, and Belle Meade to the west. This was the affluent part of town, although my parents did not entirely fit the profile. Our house had been assembled piecemeal to meet the needs of each owner for over 100 years. It had a tin roof. Sections of the house were made of log, and another wing had wooden siding which my mother painted a color called "Irish Cream." Our home was a fixer-upper when my parents bought it in 1975, a crooked anomaly perched above a sea of tidy brick and shingles.

Shortly after my birthday, I decided I was old enough to jump off the high dive at the Wildwood Swim and Tennis Club, where we were members. The jump was exhilarating, of course, but what I loved was climbing to the top of the high dive, walking out to the end of that 18-inch wide fiberglass plank, and surveying my city. The cool gorge of the Harpeth River, separated from the pool by a chain link fence, breathed softly at my back. Clear blue water beckoned just past my toes.

From the high dive I looked over the clubhouse and the tennis courts to the deep green ridges of Forest Hills. I could see the winding pavement we'd followed to the pool, the soft, manicured yards, someone's rose garden, a few remaining cow pastures, the square hedges that surrounded each long, brick rancher, an occasional oasis of aqua blue in someone's backyard. I couldn't get enough of seeing my world this way, all the green and houses, and often stood suspended in space for so long that the lifeguard would climb up to rescue me. Each time I jumped, I kept my eyes open for as long as possible, savoring the blur of sky, ridge, and brick, watching each color disappear until the water closed over my head.

That spring, my mother had taken a public relations job downtown and my father had set up his consulting firm in a spare bedroom. We possessed one reliable car, a brown VW Rabbit, and one sub-functional Peugeot wagon. Occasionally, my father, sister and I drove through the city in the Rabbit to pick up my stranded mother. There were no sidewalks in our part of town, which was mainly settled during those optimistic post-war, suburban expansion years when the automobile was the ultimate mobility solution.

I sat up front with one arm out the window, catching humid air and asphalt heat waves in my palm, watching the colors flash past my window—shade trees, children's toys, a grove of bamboo, the streets often bordered by gray stone "slave walls." Then, sidewalks appeared, the yards grew smaller then disappeared; we passed grocery stores with bars on the windows, towering housing projects, and hollowed-out buildings. I saw then, but did not understand, that Nashville was a city of marked contrasts and deep divisions.

The best part of that summer, the reason it resonates still in my family's collective memory, came early in August. My father and I discovered a thick vine dangling from a tree in the lower portion of the yard. Wooden, not at all pliable and green like the ones in cartoons, I had to ask Dad what it was. He swung out on it first to test it with his weight. Then, he handed the vine to me, closed his hands over my own to ensure my grip was tight, and let go. I pushed off a tree root and swung out over an embankment. Evening's colors—pink, green, and a misty grey—blurred around me as I flew out in an arc.

The vine became my favorite part of the yard. August in Nashville means it's too hot to play outside during the day, but after supper the air grows heavy and cool, and my father and I ventured down to swing those evenings. I invited friends over, and soon they just seemed to materialize out of every dusk. Jason, an auburn-haired boy I'd made friends with at camp, came the most. I was a bit of a risk-taker, but Jason was truly fearless. Unlike other boys I played with, he did not make fun of me for being a girl. He never walked away and left me at the top of a wall I refused to jump from, or at the mouth of a culvert I wouldn't crawl through; he simply waited for me to follow him, and I always did.

When we swung on the vine that August, it was Jason who decided that the tame step off the tree root had become boring. We started pushing the boundaries of gravity and judgement—grabbing the vine in a flying leap, pulling it backwards until it was taut and then jumping, releasing the vine mid-arc so that we soared up for a moment before crashing to the grass. By the time I started school, my hands were as callused as a day laborer's. We'd swing until our forearms spasmed, and we could no longer grip the vine properly. Then I'd lie on my back and feel the warm earth exhaling the day. My arms were soft and pale. In the fading light, I could just make out criss-crossed pink scratches and mosquito bites.

That was the last summer I could look at my glowing white skin and not understand the significance of its color. In first grade, I learned that a place I loved could be both magnificent and ugly. Jason learned, too. Even in the 1980s, desegregation disputes were shaping Nashville, determining the lives of its schoolchildren, taking us in different directions. Only now am I beginning to understand the extent to which racism shaped the path of my life, even as a grade school student in Nashville, 30 years after *Brown v. Board of Education*.

## "GOD IS THE AUTHOR...", 2005

I'm 27 now. My parents have moved to Florida, and I have to stay with friends when I visit my hometown. While my friends work, I haunt and wander. This summer, I returned again and again to the Civil Rights Collection at the downtown library. The library, finished in 2002, is a throwback to those magnificent public buildings of the early twentieth century—with marble floors, wood-paneled walls, and towering entryways. The Civil Rights Collection, in a wing off the Nashville Room, centers on a circular "lunch counter" of wood and granite where visitors can sit on stools and read a timeline of the civil rights struggle.

Veterans of the Movement attended the dedication ceremony in early 2003. John Lewis, once a student at an unaccredited black Bible college in the city, now a Georgia Congressman, teared up when he first saw the room, stacked floor to ceiling with books and decorated with photographs of him and his peers fighting the Establishment in the 1960s. Anyone who walks into the wing will understand instantly what Nashville wants visitors to know. Turn left, away from the commanding view of the State Capitol Building, and, just above the mock lunch counter, you will see a glass wall with these words inscribed upon it:

> *I have come to Nashville, not to bring inspiration,*
> *but to gain inspiration from the great movement*
> *that has taken place in this community.*
> —Martin Luther King

The "great movement" King referred to took root in the very spot where the library is located. When I browse through the Civil Rights Collection, I am on the city block where Cain-Sloan, Harvey's, and the Tic-Toc Restaurant once stood. The sit-in movement that quickly spread across the country began in those cafeterias. Well, technically, the first sit-ins occurred in Greensboro, North Carolina, on February 1, 1960, but the first *organized* sit-ins took place in Nashville five days later. The students from Fisk University, Tennessee A&I, and the American Baptist College who integrated Nashville's lunch counters had studied non-violent tactics and evaluated potential targets for months before they marched downtown and took their seats. Led by Jim Lawson, who was one of the first blacks to enroll at the Vanderbilt Divinity School, the young protestors later took leadership roles in the Freedom Rides, the marches to Montgomery, and the Student Non-Violent Coordinating Committee.

Nashvillians today, particularly older white ones, love to trumpet the progressive attitude the city adopted in the 1960s. Nashville had black councilmen and police officers while Mississippi was still under what amounted to white totalitarian rule, while black children were still being attacked by police dogs in Birmingham. At the Civil Rights Collection, visitors can sit in a soundproof glass booth and watch an episode of the PBS series *Eyes on the Prize*, entitled "Ain't Scared of Your Jails." It tells the story of Lawson, Lewis, Diane Nash, Jim Bevel, and other activists who began their work in the Movement as college students fighting to integrate Nashville's lunch counters and movie theaters. The film's opening montage shows a bustling 1960s street scene as the narrator calls Nashville a "genteel Southern city" and "the Athens of the South."

For the young activists, however, victory was not always certain and the city often seemed far from being refined.

King spoke of Nashville's "great movement" at Fisk the day after more than 4,000 blacks had marched to the courthouse to demand equal rights, as historian David Halberstam describes in his 1998 book *The Children*. The students had been sitting in for over three months with limited success; some of them had been beaten and jailed. Mayor Ben West came out to meet the crowd as they reached the courthouse steps. As cameras rolled, Nash, a Fisk student, asked the mayor, "Mr. West, don't you think it is wrong that people should be discriminated against solely on the basis of the color of their skin?"

Up to that point in his career, West had relied on highly crafted political rhetoric to satisfy moderates of both races. But that spring morning, caught off-guard and surrounded by thousands of students demanding their civil rights, West answered from his heart, "Yes, I appeal to all citizens to end discrimination, to have no bigotry, no bias, no hatred." Most of the lunch counters in downtown Nashville were integrated in the weeks following West's speech.

Today, a plaque inscribed with words from the Book of Joshua, "And the people shouted with a great shout; so that the wall fell down," commemorates the demonstration on the courthouse steps. But, like most of history's sound bites, the story of the confrontation between Nashville's mayor and Nashville's black students is isolated in memory, kept separate from the events it followed and preceded. West jettisoned his ties with the moderates that day. He was not re-elected. The march itself, though nonviolent, had been instigated by a violent event. The students had mobilized early that morning after receiving news that the home of a prominent black attorney, Z. Alexander Looby, had been dynamited. Looby and his wife were not hurt, but half their house was destroyed and the blast was so powerful it blew out most of the windows at the black medical school across the street.

Despite West's appeal to the citizens of Nashville in the spring of 1960, the bombing of Looby's house was a skirmish in a battle in a war that has yet to end. Looby was a lead attorney in a lawsuit to desegregate Nashville public schools. That suit, *Kelly v. the Board of Education*, was opened in 1955 and has never been completely put to rest. The school desegregation battle is also documented in the Civil Rights Room. A visitor who faces King's words can turn to the left, look up, and see a photograph that marks my hometown's divided past. Two black first-graders in crisp dresses, holding hands, walk past a line of people on a dirt sidewalk. A stern, protective mother walks alongside them. The crowd is white and threatening.

Here, my memory of the photograph becomes a composite of every picture I've seen of that day. Whites yelling so violently that their faces contort with the effort. A child on the verge of tears passing the mob. An angry woman holding a sign: "GOD is the AUTHOR of SEGREGATION." It is September 9, 1957, the day that 13 black first-graders entered the doors of five previously all-white schools. The photographs ran in the afternoon paper. At about three o'clock the following morning, someone threw dynamite into Hattie Cotton Elementary, and destroyed an entire wing of the building. The bombing was the first post-*Brown* violence in the country. Nashvillians side-step any mention of this dubious honor and instead harp on the actions of the city's police chief, who stood in front of the rubble and vowed that the perpetrators would be prosecuted to the fullest extent of the law. But whoever bombed Hattie Cotton was never arrested.

After a day reading in the Civil Rights Collection, I was surprised, walking outside, to see automobiles without tail fins. That evening I sat with my friends on the back porch of yet another brick rancher. The air was thick as cool soup; lightning bugs rose from a yard so green it was almost painful to look at. We sipped bourbon and Coke. I told my friend Lelia, a schoolteacher and longtime friend from church, about the woman invoking God in the photograph.

"Wow," she said. "You know, you just wonder what that person must think today when they see themselves in a picture like that."

Truth is, I hadn't wondered. But Lelia was right. The children walking to school that day were about the same age as my mother. I still have two living grandparents. That woman might still be out there somewhere. Perhaps she was, like me, enjoying the summer evening, drink in hand, in a house on a street named after a Confederate general. Did she attend her grandchildren's high school graduations and press her lips into an angry pink line whenever black, Laotian, or Hispanic kids got their diplomas? Maybe she thought of her sign, covered in plastic and waiting, deep in a corner of the guest room closet.

Or maybe it is as Lelia suggests—the woman is ashamed. She burned the sign. She refuses to go on trips to the library with her Sunday School friends. She thanks God that her face is not really visible in the photograph and she keeps her hair in a different style now. Nashville has come so far since that day that virtually everyone who sees the myriad photographs of angry whites threatening frightened children and stoic mothers feels a sense of revulsion. But the foundation for intolerance, for co-existence without acceptance, was laid. Each subsequent generation has either built upon it or torn it down, usually some combination of the two. Like me, perhaps the woman in the photograph knows that there has been no clear winner in the battle begun that day.

## SOUTHERN MANIFESTOS, 1955-1971

The black children attending a handful of white public schools that distant autumn were all first graders. As they walked to their new schools that day, they might also have been remembering a dream summer. In many ways, I couldn't be more distant from the two girls holding hands in the photograph I am so drawn to. But those children are about the same age as my parents, and childhood does share some transcendent joys. I can imagine some things. Hula Hoops were not on the scene yet, but there were jacks, jump rope, and The Coasters. When those diversions grew tiresome, the girls might have gone to the Ritz Theatre in the heart of black Nashville and watched *Cinderella* or a Jerry Lewis movie. The early Civil Rights Movement had its roots in the church and no church anywhere in the South can go a summer without holding a potluck supper. So the girls may have gone to some. Their picnics would not have been at the swim clubs or public parks where I had mine, but I imagine they might have had fried chicken and coconut cake just like my church and perhaps found a grassy area to play tag.

Of course, there is also the matter of back-to-school shopping. Clothing was important in the black community, particularly for anyone who was setting out to challenge the white establishment. The girls would have gone downtown and purchased brand-new Sunday clothes to wear on that harrowing first day. In the photograph, the dresses look frilly and starched. They probably tried on innumerable swaths of itchy lace before their mothers decided on the perfect outfit. They probably got hungry and grouchy. There would have been no place for them to sit down and eat lunch, and in most stores there wouldn't have been bathrooms for them.

All the children who integrated the city's schools in 1957 were first graders because Nashville had adopted a grade-a-year desegregation plan in response, not to the 1954 *Brown v. the Board of Education* decision, but to *Kelly v. the Board of Education*. *Kelly* was filed in Nashville courts when Robert Kelly's teenage son had been turned away from the doors of all-white East High School on the first day of school in 1955. (A detailed account of Nashville's busing era can be found in a 1985 book, *The Burden of Busing*, by Richard Pride and J. David Woodard.) Most reigning Nashville officials were pleased with the plan to desegregate schools grade-by-grade. They believed that its value lay in the gradual introduction of desegregation. It was also optional, which proponents claimed was respectful of freedom of choice and did not require the reorganization of neighborhood schools. The Nashville Plan, as it was dubbed, was subsequently adopted by post-*Brown* communities across the country.

Black leaders were dubious of the grade-a-year approach. Desegregation under the Nashville Plan would not be "complete" until 1968. Looby and his partner, NAACP attorney Avon Williams, said that the gradual introduction would give white Nashvillians plenty of time to re-settle in the suburbs.

Williams was right. After *Brown*, schools opened all along Nashville's outer ring. Officially, this was to deal with the baby boom population, but the timing and placement gave wealthy families plenty of time to get their children into a school that was not likely to desegregate. One of these, Percy Priest Elementary School, was built in 1957, ahead of the population boom in Forest Hills. Percy Priest himself was a beloved New Deal Congressman. In March 1956, Priest and other lawmakers, including both Tennessee senators, refused to sign the Southern Manifesto, a document written by Southern members of Congress vowing to fight *Brown* and desegregation. Ironically, the school that bears Priest's name did not have a single black student until busing-for-racial-balance began in 1971.

Percy Priest Elementary was constructed in my neighborhood as the farmland was being subdivided ahead of an expected population boom. The street names, chosen by developers and early residents, were a Southern Manifesto in their own right: Robert E. Lee, Jefferson Davis, Merimac, Confederate, and General Bedford Forrest. Early settlers of my neighborhood were hunkering down, fending off a perceived invasion. I was nine or ten, studying the Civil War in Social Studies class, before I realized that these names meant anything but the route to church, a street for bike stunts, and my friends' addresses. With each school year, as our study of the Civil War progressed, I learned to recognize more Confederate Street names—Beauregard, Fredericksburg, Stonewall Jackson, Hood's Hill, Benton Smith. With each name added to the list, I felt a complex sadness. I am a part of a generation of white Southerners, arguably the first, who had to be told that systemic segregation had once dominated our society. We thought it was over, left in the past, an epic battle of good and evil in which good had prevailed. Instead, Southerners who were still my neighbors *had* taken a stand against desegregation. I was, daily, travelling the paths they had named.

## FOREST HILLS AND BUSING, 1971-1984

The Civil Rights Collection adjoins the Nashville Room, where old people come with tote bags full of pencils and spiral notebooks to research their genealogy. There are shelves of hardcover books with histories of towns, schools, and churches around Middle Tennessee. A few of these interested me—like the history of Beersheba Springs, a mountain town known for the Methodist Assembly at its center; Maury County, where I worked as a reporter; and Hume-Fogg High School, the first public high school in the county and my alma mater. When I wasn't in the Civil

Rights Collection, I was either skimming those books or eating lunch on the first floor. The café, with its windows facing Church Street, was perfect for watching pedestrians. I'd also notice all the people eating lunch around me—black, white, Asian, Hispanic; business lunches, mothers' groups, retirees.

The hallways between the Nashville Room and the café were lined with photographs of established Nashville images like the Ryman Auditorium, Tootsie's Orchid Lounge, the stage of the Grand Ole Opry, mist rising off the Cumberland River below the skyline, the city's full-scale replica of the Parthenon surrounded by fall foliage. One picture in this glossy collection made me stop dead the first time I noticed it:

It's a picture of my fourth grade class, or at least a portion of it. I recognize a few of the faces, the trapezoidal tables, and the topographical maps behind them. Actually, the photograph is an amalgam of several classrooms, put together to showcase ethnic diversity. All of the white children in the shot, except for a towheaded boy, have dark eyes and hair. There is an Asian girl raising her hand with gusto and two black children, including my old first-grade friend, Marc, in the back row. I remember, vaguely, the day a professional came to take those photographs for the superintendent's office. During the shoot most of us white kids played games in another classroom, jumping slightly at each pop of the big flash.

This photograph wants to bury the image of screaming protestors and replace it with a spectrum of color. But back then we had no idea what we represented, or what we were overcoming. We didn't know that the diversity we experienced every day was the result of a concentrated effort to desegregate the schools, just as that picture was an effort to present a classroom full of happy, racially tolerant children. I laughed a little when I saw the photograph hanging as a celebration of Nashville in the new public library. To discover how these faces had been brought together in a classroom, I only had to walk back to the Nashville Room, open a filing cabinet, and begin reading newspaper clippings from the 1970s. Here there are more angry parents. The children crossing picket lines are both white and black. **BUSING BEGINS**, one headline screams. There is a hint of panic and confusion in the faces, of resignation in the articles. Busing had come to Nashville.

Congressman Priest died a year before the ribbon cutting for his namesake school, a long, one-story building across the street from acres of woods, about 10 miles from downtown. The school had a horseshoe driveway bordered by oak saplings. Those trees had grown enough to create a tunnel effect when my father turned up the driveway to take me to first grade in August 1984. When I arrived, the school was just emerging from years of being under threat of closure. So many families left public schools after busing began that the entire school system had been thrown into turmoil.

The optional grade-a-year plan, which was Nashville's official policy through the '50s and '60s, was ineffective. Due to the zoning system, by 1960 only 44 black children were enrolled in white city schools, and none of the county schools were racially mixed. Because Nashville's neighborhoods were segregated, its schools were, as well. In 1969, 14 years after *Kelly V. Board of Education*, long after the children it was filed for would have left public schools, and after the notorious Nashville Plan had run its course, the original plaintiffs in Kelly filed a brief with the U.S. District Court. The plaintiffs requested that a plan be devised to put an 80/20 white/black ratio in all schools in the city and county—which had become the consolidated Metropolitan-Davidson County government in 1964. According to the 1970 census, Davidson County was 20 percent black. However, only 19 of 125 schools in the county were between 15 and 35 percent black. In the fall of 1971, busing was implemented to establish a balance that reflected the actual race ratio of the county.

Busing began a new era of racial division in Nashville. Black children bore the majority of the travel burden. They had to leave their neighborhoods downtown and in the eastern portion of the city for hour-long rides out to suburban elementary and high schools. Whites were only bused to the inner city for middle school, but their complaints, which they euphemistically called "safety concerns," were the loudest. The busing plan, though hurried into action, would have been stable enough were it not for the racism and economic clout of whites in outlying areas of the city. From the 1960s to the mid-1980s, 18 church-sponsored private schools opened to accommodate whites who did not want their children to be bused. Percy Priest's enrollment dropped from 450 in 1971 to just over 100 in 1981.

But busing also gave the city a chance to break down racial barriers. White parents who supported the mission of the public schools went door-to-door handing out flyers to recruit kindergartners. Becky Long, whose youngest daughter became a classmate of mine, talked to my parents while I was still in preschool. Because of that conversation, I was one of 18 five-year-olds who began kindergarten at Percy Priest in 1983. Kindergartners were not bused. There was one black child in my class.

Like Mrs. Long, my mom and dad became advocates for public schools throughout the '80s and '90s. I recently interviewed Mrs. Long and asked her why she'd spoken up for Percy Priest and sent all three of her children there.

"Nashville was just so anti-black, I thought, and a lot of it still is. There were just families who did not want their children going to school with poor black kids and there was that undercurrent here. But there was a core neighborhood group who believed in public schools."

## THE CLASS OF VAN WHITTAKER, 1984

The halls at Percy Priest were green and yellow and smelled like paste. I was adrift in a sea of backpacks and chatter, buoyed along by my father's hand. Adults were operating about two-and–a-half feet above my head; waists and belts; Southern accents greeting each other, handshakes. All of it a cacophony. I felt my father's wedding band against the inside of my knuckle and pulled him over to the class lists.

At my level, someone shrieked with delight, "I got Mrs. Kennedy!"

Mrs. Kennedy was definitely the first grade teacher of choice. Tall, with grandmotherly salt and pepper curls, her reading glasses dangled from a delicate chain around her neck. The other teacher, Mrs. Whittaker, had been universally feared by the kindergartners. I would later realize that she spoke very loudly when she became passionate about something. The year before, however, we just thought Mrs. Whittaker enjoyed screaming at her students. We could hear her from our classroom across the hall. I was terrified of her and made a point of avoiding eye contact.

My name was on her class list, in red marker on tablet paper, printed neatly above Welch, Andrea. It would be an exaggeration to say that my life flashed before my eyes. Only my summer did—the feel of a saddle between my knees, sherbet and cake, blur and splash of water, soaring from the vine. All of it gone and me staring at my name printed in red below the name of a teacher who I was pretty sure hated kids. I looked down the hallway for the closest exit, but could only see a swirling mass of six- and seven-year-olds. I was trapped. My father was still holding my hand, and he shook it sideways.

"Look, right here, Erin. It says you're in Mrs. Whittaker's class; do you want to find the room?"

"Dad," I croaked.

And suddenly she was there, purple pants first, then hands on her knees, then a face looking into mine. She didn't look frightening, more owl-like than anything, with round glasses and warm brown skin.

"Hello, Erin! I'm so glad to have you in my class this year!"

If this was designed to comfort me, it had the opposite effect. How did she know my name when I'd spent an entire school year trying to stay off her radar? And why was she glad to have me? In kindergarten, rule-following had not been one of my virtues. I was overly talkative. I never slept during naps. I daydreamed so much that I occasionally wandered into other class lines and got lost in the school. I wrapped myself around my father's leg.

"She's shy," he lied.

They talked for a while, Dad and Mrs. Whittaker. I tried not to cry. Dad came down to my level and hugged me goodbye. Then his Duck Heads disappeared into the sea of khakis, jeans, and skirts. I summoned some of the bravery that had taken me off the high dive and walked into my new classroom.

Our class was huge. I wondered where all my classmates had been the year before. I knew only a few children from my kindergarten class, but Jason was there. About 10 of my new classmates were black. I had seen lots of black kids filing out of the line of buses in the driveway, but had given it little thought. My friends would be the kids who preferred the swings to any other piece of playground equipment. I was glad to see Jason there, and more than a little surprised. I'd come to expect my friends from camp, church, and the pool to be private school kids.

I'd known about private schools since preschool, when my closest friend's parents decided to send her to Harding Academy for kindergarten, but I was in high school before I fully understood why they existed. While I was arguing with my father about whether or not racism was still a factor in daily life (I thought it wasn't), he told me about picking me up from Jason's house after that first day of first grade. While my friend and I watched "He-Man" in the den, Jason's parents pulled Dad aside in the kitchen and, leaning against the counters with their arms crossed, began a hasty conversation about Mrs. Whittaker.

"You've seen her," they told my father. "What are we going to do?"

Dad played dumb.

"What do you mean?" he asked.

He hadn't taken their secret handshake, so Jason's parents back-pedaled and swung into a technical discussion about academics and test scores. By the end of the week, Jason had left Percy Priest and gone to

The Oak Hill School, a private Presbyterian academy run by the same people who were in charge of the day camp. I added Jason to a list of neighborhood friends going to private schools. Children in Forest Hills allied themselves with public or private schools like sports teams. The public school kids were definitely the underdogs.

Mrs. Whittaker was not mean, only passionate; a social activist teaching first grade. At Halloween, she encouraged us to trick-or-treat for UNICEF instead of candy. We learned all the words to "We are the World" and sang it for a school assembly. After a few civics lessons and talks about homelessness, only five kids voted for Reagan in the class election. To teach us about disabilities, she asked us to try to push our chairs under our desks without using our arms or navigate the classroom with our eyes closed. At Christmas, we organized a school-wide clothing drive. Life, I realized, extended far beyond the simple pleasures of my neighborhood. On Martin Luther King's birthday, Mrs. Whittaker asked us, "How would you feel if you couldn't go to school with someone whose skin was not the same color as yours?"

I stopped looking out the window and searched my classroom. Aaron, Thad, and Brooke were white, and my closest friends. But there was also Cova, Hope, Keisha, and David, who ate lunch with us and were always up for a game of kickball or four square. I could live without Tessa, a wiry black girl who tormented me for fun, but she was easy enough to avoid. Mrs. Whittaker was a good teacher. Mrs. Murphy was also black and she taught P.E., which was by far the best class of the day. This question our teacher had asked, well, it was absurd. I couldn't imagine a school with only white people.

"What if I told you that it used to be like that?" she asked. "Because, it did, you know. People used to believe that black people and white people were different and that blacks were not as good as whites. It was the law that black and white children be separated. Some people still believe that."

For the rest of the day, we talked about the civil rights movement and the racism that had made the movement necessary. Mrs. Whittaker had a slide show and a *Weekly Reader* devoted to the topic. The slide show was one of those beeping film strips with a narrator. Black students at a lunch counter with mustard on their heads, white toughs in the background. Beep. Women and children crossing a massive bridge while State Troopers with billy clubs waited on the other side. Beep. Martin Luther King speaking in front of a sea of people. Beep. Many of the youngest marchers were about the same age as our parents. This was not ancient history.

The *Weekly Reader* had a picture of two water fountains, the nicer one designated for whites, a smaller one with the word "colored" above it. The caption beneath had a word I recognized: "N-a-s-h-v-i-l-l-e." My city. A picture of women and children knocked down by fire hoses said, "Birmingham." My grandmother's city. It was hard enough to learn that these things had taken place, but discovering that they occurred in places I knew and loved made it nearly impossible to understand.

I was six. I didn't leave school that day filled with anger. I didn't vow to fight racism, but questions had been raised. They grew more sophisticated over time until I found myself holed up in the library this summer, squinting over newspaper articles and photographs, hoping that acceptable answers about my city would somehow form before me if I only read enough.

## THE NEXT SUMMER, 1985

I don't know much about the black first graders from 1957; that's not surprising. What's troubling is that I know virtually nothing about the black first graders from my class. I have no idea what happened to them. I can hardly remember first and last names. Even when I was in school with them every day, I knew remarkably little about their lives. We went to school together and played together there, but they all climbed onto buses at the end of the day and went home. In the evenings, when I was going to Girl Scouts, children's choir, and Little League, the black kids weren't around. I knew that most of them came to school long before I did in the morning and ate breakfast in the school cafeteria. This fascinated me. When I was six, I was in love with all the trappings of elementary school—lunch boxes, pencil sharpeners, milk tickets, school bus rides. Hope and David said I was crazy for wanting to ride the school bus. I told them not only did I want to ride the bus, I wanted to eat breakfast at the school like they did. One day, my mother finally relented. With three quarters clenched in my fist, I caught the first school bus that went past my house that morning. It was still misty outside. "What are you doing here?" David asked me.

"I want to eat breakfast at the school," I said.

"Girl, you're crazy," he said back.

Breakfast consisted of a piece of dry French toast floating in some substance masquerading as maple syrup. The fruit of the day was cantaloupe, which I hated. The cafeteria was full and loud. I was the only white person in the room. I felt like an intruder. David was a veteran. He wrapped his French toast around his cantaloupe like a taco and dipped it into the maple syrup.

"What do you think?" he asked me.

"It's not bad," I said.

"Liar," he said, with his mouth full.

I fell asleep in class that morning and had to stand in a corner. My stomach was growling. While the class watched a filmstrip, I snuck into my lunch box and ate all the 'Nilla Wafers.

By the summer of 1985, I was beginning to understand and navigate the divides in my city. At Oak Hill Day Camp, Jason wouldn't play with me. He told me we were too different now, going to public and private schools. I was hurt, enraged. Between the two of us, we managed to divide the entire second-grade camp into public and private school factions, splitting that way into teams for battle ball and relay races.

After camp ended, my father announced that he could run a business with a six-year-old and a one-year-old underfoot but not a seven-year-old and a two-year-old. So Cathleen and I were sent to day care three days a week. Cathleen went to the program at our church and I went to Percy Priest. Day care was a ceaseless arrangement of field trips, rented movies, and board game tournaments. It was bearable enough, but I also found it exhausting to be in school without the comfortable schedules, divisions, and rules that I'd come to expect from Mrs. Whittaker.

Sue, the day care director, decided to take us swimming every week. There were no public pools in our part of town. Like my own, all the families belonged to swim and tennis clubs. The closest municipal pool was at Rose Park on the periphery of the Edgehill housing projects. Sue gave a little speech about us being guests at this pool. She told us we would stand out, but that we went to school with a lot of these kids, so it shouldn't be a big deal. I didn't listen very closely. I had just come from a year in Mrs. Whittaker's class, after all, and I thought I understood.

Looking back on my first day at Rose Park, I don't think my problems arose because I was white; I think they came up because I was *so* white—carved from bone, my hair like corn silk. I ran up to the pool and jumped in. When I came up, I expected to find David or Cova. Instead, I was surrounded by a sea of older kids I'd never seen before.

"Who are *you*?" they asked. "What are you doing here?"

"I'm swimming with my day care," I said, ducking under the water again.

When I came up in another spot, I was alone, which I preferred whenever I swam. But it wasn't long before I was surrounded again. I couldn't figure out what was going on, why kids I didn't know seemed to be following me. Fed up, I pulled my arms back and shoved my hands through the water, splashing everyone within 10 feet, hoping everyone would scatter. What followed was not exactly a fight, just extremely rough play with kids who were older, bigger, and tougher than I was. I was blinded by spray, I collided with people when I tried to swim away, and then someone started dunking me. Between breaths, I worked my way to the edge of the pool, climbed out, and ran. The lifeguard yelled at me just as I collided with a railing, stubbed my toe, and skinned my knuckles. "That's why you shouldn't run," he said, towering over me.

I hobbled over to a chaise lounge and refused to get back into the water. The Rose Park kids and the day care kids united to taunt me. At the end of the day, walking barefoot to the van just as I always did at Wildwood, I stepped on broken glass. Howling with pain and anger as Sue picked the crystal shards glistening with blood from the bottoms of my feet, I vowed that I would never return to Rose Park.

The next Wednesday, just as I was starting in on a bowl of Wheaties, the phone rang. My mother handed it to me, looking smug. It was Sue. I knew this call had been pre-arranged.

"Erin, please come with us to Rose Park today. You don't have to be afraid of the black kids," she said.

I bristled at the accusation. "I'm not afraid of black kids, but the kids at Rose Park are mean."

"They're not mean," Sue said, "You just seem so different to them."

"But blacks and whites aren't supposed to be different," I said in a pitch-perfect recitation of what I believed Mrs. Whittaker had taught us. "That's wrong. Only the bad guys thought they were different."

Sue wasn't sure how to reason with me. "Look, what would you do if you were at your pool and a black girl just ran up and jumped in? Wouldn't you be interested in her?"

"I wouldn't hold her head underwater," I said. "Besides, it isn't the black kids. I don't want to go to Rose Park because of the glass."

"Well, your mother says you don't have to go if you don't want to."

"I don't."

"Okay, then, we'll miss you. Please think about it for next week," Sue said.

"Bye," I said.

I spent the morning lying on my bed, propped on my elbows, looking out the window at my woods and the rolling green hillside. I could walk barefoot all day in my yard with nothing worse to worry about than bee stings. The fact that I didn't want to go back to Rose Park scared me as much as the place itself. I *was* afraid of the people there, and all the people there were black. I finally decided to return weeks later, not out of any conviction, but because I didn't feel like I could come up with an acceptable reason for my fear. I never had fun there. Every time I went to Rose Park, I'd sit in a shady corner of the patio or wade gingerly around the pool, as though I could step on glass at any moment. I longed for Wildwood, where I could climb the high dive and be familiar with all that I surveyed.

## WE SPEAK OF THE PAST, 2005

It would be unfair to say that everyone who sent their child to a private school in Nashville was like Jason's family. By the time my friends and I started first grade, the private schools were a decade past their founding. They had their own merits by then and most were no longer meeting in hastily converted Sunday School classrooms. Besides, busing was not working as well as people had hoped it would. Because of the constant fluxes in the white population, zoning lines were frequently redrawn. Children were forced to change schools every year, so more and more parents, desiring stability, were pulling their kids out of public schools, exacerbating the problem for those who remained.

Most of my current friends in Nashville are the ones who grew up in the same church as I did. Nearly all of them went to private schools. I was hesitant to talk about my research while I was home over the summer, afraid that I would offend them. However, all of my friends were interested. Everyone could recall a time when some truth about Nashville's racial divides had become apparent.

In 1998, two years after I graduated from high school, busing for racial balance was eliminated from Metro-Nashville Public Schools. Busing was a flawed system, yes, but without it the city is retreating again into its separate enclaves. My friend Kris notices it in the youth group he leads every Sunday. The kids seem less aware of their role in a larger city, of the other cultures within it. When they cross town, they make jokes about getting shot.

"What can we do?" I asked Kris one morning before heading to the library.

"Education, I suppose," he said. "Just keep exposing them to different people and places."

I agreed, but in a sense, that answer is too simple. Educating the younger generation simply hands them the ball. *It's your problem now.* We learned that from busing. I learned that race was a problem bigger than friendship as a child at the Rose Park pool. How can my city be as whole and beautiful as I'd believed it to be when I was six? I'd hoped, as I pored over material in the Civil Rights Collection, that some answer would present itself to me. It didn't, but as I turned to leave on my last day in town, I noticed an inscription over the doorway, words spoken by John Lewis to rally the Freedom Riders in 1961:

*If not us, then who? If not now, then when?*

# WHAT TREES BECOME

### TABLES AND CHAIRS

I f we are formed by what we love, how does the actual shape of places we've loved create and mold us? Are we aware when it happens? As I write this, I'm sitting at the kitchen table in my attic apartment, watching traffic on U.S. 19 into Morgantown, West Virginia. My table is a red-toned wooden drop-leaf. The chairs are ladderback with woven cane seats, made from wood slightly more yellow than the table's. The table fits nicely in a corner by the window—my perch above the passing world. My apartment is small, but comfortable. As an adult, I can behave and fit into this space as if it's always been just me, independent. However, the table reveals the truth. In the late afternoon light, once I've cleared all the magazines, newspapers, and my stack of work from its top before dinner, it's easy to see four spots worn smooth by decades of plates and elbows. For 20 years, this was the breakfast table in my family home.

My parents moved to Florida last summer. I was between teaching jobs so I went home to Nashville to help them pack. I emptied all the shelves and cabinets, covered the floor with U-Haul boxes, but didn't really register that my family was leaving the home where I'd grown up until my mother offered the table from the kitchen.

"You know, Erin," she said, "You can have the kitchen table for your new apartment."

I was seated at the dining room table, my toes curled around a rung on my ladderback chair. "You won't need it?" I asked.

"No, the new house is pretty small."

I wanted to resist, but I was near-broke and worried about furniture.

"Umm, yeah. I guess I'll take it."

"Take those chairs, too."

"The *ladderback chairs*? Why?"

"Well, they've never really matched the dining room table. We'll get new ones in Florida."

"They've been here for forever. Of course they match."

"No, Erin, really, they don't. Look, I can't talk about this now," Mom kissed me on the forehead and left for work.

I listened to the familiar sound of her car downshifting to descend our steep driveway and looked at the table and chairs. Mom was right. The chairs were Shaker-style and the dining room table was dark walnut with ornate carved patterns adorning the legs. They didn't match, yet I couldn't imagine them separated. How many meals had we shared in this mis-matched space? We ate supper as a family every night of the workweek. Even if we had to eat at 5:00, even if we were so mad at each other we could barely speak, we ate together. And suddenly, the table would be in Florida, the chairs in West Virginia. The dining room had absorbed all our conversation and teasing, the scrape of knives and forks, the shimmy and creak of the wooden table as someone leapt up to retrieve forgotten butter or salt from the kitchen, and it would never again be filled with those noises. I stood up and paced around the room, attempting to visualize the things I would never see again. My parents still had the ridiculous brass chandelier they'd talked about getting rid of for as long as I could remember. I sat down at my spot and tried to picture my father across from me, my mother to my left, my sister to my right. What had we talked about all those nights? The familiar was too familiar, simply a blur. With nothing left to see, I leaned forward in my chair in that half-packed house and studied the tiny flecks of wood grain in the table—the way they were softened, then magnified, by my tears.

## WALLS AND FLOORS

My father told me over the phone that their new house was a bungalow. I'd pictured faded blue wooden siding on a house that was perhaps settling into the sandy earth a little faster on one side than the other. I always imagine my family living amid disarray, as though our personalities project themselves into physicality, but the house in Florida is square and brick. I first saw it on a night in June, having driven from Nashville with a car full of Christmas ornaments and other items Mom didn't trust the movers with. I listened to the car cooling off, rested my chin on the steering wheel, and wondered how my family could ever fill such a space.

Growing up, everyone around us lived in brick ranchers built in the '50s and '60s. Our home was part log, part cream-colored wooden siding, and constructed in stages between 1900 and 1960. The process must have been a little pell-mell. My parents once removed dry wall in the 1960 addition only to find that there weren't any studs holding up the windows. My father called to tell me about the miraculous floating wall and said, "Our house is really more of a good idea for a building than an actual building."

My sister Cathleen and I both grew up in that good idea for a house at the lyrical address of 1330 Otter Creek Road. Say it. Feel the alliteration? coming off your tongue, then consider the images—a playful animal, a shady creek, summer shadows, green and blue. If you like, you can add Nashville, Tennessee, and think of dreams and music. Is it any wonder that Cathleen and I are both in love with words and images? More of a good idea than an actual place. Flawed, yes, but beautiful for it.

Winters, Cathleen and I used empty margarine tubs and yardsticks to play hockey in our sock feet, gliding around the living room and dining room floors. The hardwood was always cool in the summer and freezing in the winter, but I never wore slippers. I liked the texture of the floor, the way the wood was smooth if I walked with the grain, rough if I walked across it, and every couple of inches there was a tiny gap between the floorboards. During summer vacations in junior high, I liked to pull out my parents' LPs, lie on the cool floor in front of the speakers, and listen to *McCartney* or *Magical Mystery Tour* over and over. When I was about three, I had a push car that I rode off the two-inch steps between each room, streaking across the dining room and into the kitchen on what I called "the hill," which was actually a spot where hackberry roots had pushed up the floor.

I remember 1330 as those dark hardwood floors and strawberry-blonde log walls with white chinking in between. Some of my childhood friends thought we lived in a gingerbread house. At night, the logs reflected ambient light and, from the outside, our house did glow like it was part of a model Christmas village. 1330 Otter Creek Road. Sounds carried through our house as well as light. I could lie on the couch before supper while the rest of my family was upstairs and read their moods just by listening to their voices and watching the ceiling shift with their footsteps. Because you can't be quiet in a house where your mood reverberates through the floors, we never tried. We were loud in anger and joy. We called to each other through the ceilings and vents, relished equally the rapid taps our footsteps made if we ran down the stairs excitedly and the high wooden echo of a door slammed in anger. Every place I have lived since has seemed dark and flat in comparison.

I was fascinated by the quiet of my friends' houses when I was a child. When I was very young, I called them "real houses," because, even to me, my home seemed like a fantasy or world apart. My friends' homes had long hallways and wall-to-wall carpeting. Every footfall was soft. There were no squeaky boards or errant nail heads, no shifting wood grain beneath my bare feet. Yells traveled, but didn't echo. The walls were covered in thick, textured wallpaper. My friends spent their family time in rooms called "dens," which made me think of foxes watching *Sesame Street* in their holes. What my friends called living rooms had fancy pictures on the walls, ornate chairs and couches, a piano, and china on display in the picture windows. We weren't allowed to do any actual living in living rooms. Driving through my neighborhood at night, there were dozens of those rooms, visible from the street and no one ever inside them. I couldn't understand why anyone would keep the light on in a room that was never used, or why the rooms even existed since no one was in them. My parents didn't get it either.

Mom and Dad did not want to sell our house. They didn't want to leave Nashville at all, but several lean years at my father's business forced the issue. They bought a much smaller house in Jacksonville and, for several months, convinced themselves that they would rent our family home to visiting professors or a young family. When my parents moved, they said they would only live in Jacksonville until they had enough money to retire back to that cabin on the hill. They tried to find someone to rent the house, but they couldn't even find a leasing agent to take them on as clients.

The problem is that not everyone who visits my house sees the same thing. In fact, most don't see what my family and I see—or rather, they see what has faded to background for us. The upstairs ceilings are slanted in the shape of the tin roof above them. When the sun's at the right angle, daylight shows through the chinking in the walls. The house itself is off-square. We forget to mention the steps between the rooms, and our guests always stumble. The front door jams. I always loved the squeal our door made when it caught in the jamb, and how it was followed immediately by the shudder of wood forced open by shoulder or knee and the single clack of the upset brass knocker. That sound meant arrival to me, but to a prospective realtor, it means check the foundation.

---

Mom and Dad have lived in the brick home in Jacksonville for over a year now. We ate Christmas dinner last year in green plastic chairs at the dining room table because they hadn't found wooden ones they liked. The floors are hardwood, but level and more solid than the Nashville ones. I still have not learned how to gauge anyone's mood from the sound. But, even in these new, sturdy rooms, a sense of disarray and movement has followed them.

I keep a pretty clean apartment in West Virginia, so my first entry into my parents' house is often a shock. I usually spend a couple hours sorting piles of mail, cleaning Land's End catalogues and *New Yorkers* off the old trunk they use as a coffee table, and convincing them to throw things away. After a day or two, I grow accustomed to the nature of my parents' home. I give up on sorting and organizing, and stop stubbing my toe on the exercise bike smack in the middle of their Pottery Barn living room suite. I love that the mindset imparted on us by the house at 1330 seems to follow us.

### WINDOW AND DOOR FRAMES

My parents redecorated or renovated every room in 1330 except their own bedroom. They never got around to the job and it remains a green-shagged monument to the 1970s. On the wall behind my parents' door, there's a doorknob-shaped depression in the dry wall. This is my contribution. When I was about three, my parents moved me into the only bedroom in the house with an east-facing window. I never slept past the moment the sun rose over the ridge and my room became light. Mom and Dad tried everything. I remember watching the news, *Hill Street Blues*, and Johnny Carson with them. They'd put me to bed at 11:30, but I still woke at sunrise, and the first place I headed was my parents' bedroom. Dad loves sharing this story with new parents. "No matter what we did, five a.m. would come and WHAM," Dad always extends his right arm like he's throwing open a door at this point in the story: "That *kid* would hit that *door*. It sounded like a rifle shot! I finally just installed one of those hook-and-eye locks so she couldn't get in and told her to take care of herself until we got up."

This is true and, with nothing else to do, I stood at my bedroom window and watched the sunrise, the way the light filled the sky and the sun turned the winter trees to silhouettes. I was four years old, did not yet know words like wondrous, but I knew that was what I was witnessing—the moment when night rolls over into day—carried some sort of sustaining energy, was somehow remarkable. Even now, morning is my favorite time of the day. I'm not the type of morning person who chats it up, whistles, and assaults people with joyous tidings. But I appreciate mornings as a time to think clearly and dawn as a type of resurrection.

My parents decided to sell the house in the springtime, just as I was finishing up my first year in Morgantown. Mom called early one morning to tell me. They were worn out, she said, by the strain of trying to find a tenant while paying two mortgages. It was April, the first truly beautiful week of spring. In Nashville, that sunlight was shining across the vivid green yard, shadows were moving across the empty room that had been mine.

I'd been ripped off my axis. I told Mom they hadn't tried hard enough to find someone to rent it, that selling the house was a huge mistake because they were losing a place they'd loved for three decades. In 10 years, when they realized they were stuck in a state where it was hot all the time, in a house where they could never fit their grandkids for a decent Christmas, they'd be sorry. I hung up the phone, feeling angry and vindicated, sat at my table, watched the traffic, and wept. After a while, I washed my face, poured myself a glass of water, and began to imagine a potential buyer.

Growing up, I knew others had called our house their home. The oldest portion, where my room, the kitchen, and a couple of closets were located, was built around 1900 by a wood cutter. Later, there was a man who kept some livestock and orchards. He built a little red barn I could see from my bedroom window.

Families added on and moved in during the '40s, '50s, and '60s. One man who lived there was a prominent druggist. Another operated a metal-plating business out of the barn. My dad had gathered enough neighborhood stories to learn that the woodsman probably built our house up in the woods so he could operate an illicit business or two.

A door in the back of my bedroom leads to a tiny room with a row of windows and a small door that opens right into the woods. Dad made up bedtime stories about men playing illegal poker in that room and running out the secret door into the woods whenever the sheriff came. One fall when I was going door-to-door for a school fundraiser, an older lady told me that her mother wouldn't allow her to play in the woods behind my house because of moonshiners. Sometimes I would lie in my bed touching the wall, and imagine men on the other side drinking rotgut, their faces obscured by cards and cigarette smoke. Sometimes I heard them, heard the secret knocks on the tiny door, the lock sliding, the door creaking open, rough voices muttering to each other.

It's November now and my parents still haven't been able to sell the house. They are happy in Florida. Their neighborhood has sidewalks, and people sit on their porches in the evenings. Both my parents grew up near the ocean and they've told me they don't know how they lived in a landlocked state for so long. There is little sadness about the move unless something reminds us of Nashville or one of us visits the old house. Dad went up last weekend to clean the gutters and repair the picket fence. The house is still familiar—the shape of its rooms, the way sunlight moves across the windows during the day, the sound of one's own footfalls. But it's empty. There are no one else's footsteps, no jazz or Irish music on the stereo, no one cleaning up in the kitchen, only shells of rooms that seem as familiar as breathing. I wasn't surprised when my phone rang last Saturday morning and my father sounded melancholy. He was standing in my old bedroom, looking out the window. At 7:30 on an autumn morning, I knew exactly what he was seeing.

"The sun must be streaming in," I said.

"How did you ever get any sleep in this room?" Dad asked.

Dad told me he felt as empty as the house. I reminded him that he and Mom loved standing together at the vast edge of the ocean and eating oysters on the half shell at Slider's Bar and Grill. But Dad wouldn't be cheered.

"It's forlorn up here. I feel like we've abandoned it."

"We did," I said, feeling my throat tighten. "Without us, it's just wood and glass surrounding air."

Neither of us could talk about it any more after that. It was easier to focus on the tasks of the day. Me, grading papers and writing at my table while trying not to notice the worn spots in the wood. Dad, fixing things up and meeting with the realtor. He called me again before church the next morning. He'd decided that the house smelled empty, so he'd gone to

Kroger for matches and a pound of bacon. He'd fixed a fire in the fireplace Saturday night, had coffee, bacon, and eggs for breakfast Sunday morning. The house smelled like someone lived in it. His other good news was that the newest realtor was confident she would find someone to buy the house. The trick was choosing an audience. This was not a house for the Land Rover set. This was a house for people who drove old Volvos, shopped at Wild Oats, and dressed their children in fleece and tiny Birkenstocks.

From a practical standpoint, all any of us can really hope for is that the house isn't torn down and replaced by a "replica." But I dream of more than that. I want a family to fall in love with my old house, and I want that family to include a gawky tomboy who occupies the bedroom with the slanted ceilings and east-facing window. She'll know it's daylight before she opens her eyes and then she'll get out of bed and stand in her flannels at the window. She will stand in the chill and feel her family solidly around her, perhaps hear someone turning over in bed, perhaps hear the creak of the hardwood floor as the house itself breathes. If it is spring, she will see the clover in the yard, even smell it faintly in the air around her. This child will watch the sliver of sky between the ridge tops going from blue to pink to glowing orange. She will understand luminosity before she has a word for it.

### THE WOODS AROUND US

One autumn, when I was in seventh grade and actually sleeping in on the weekends, my father woke me up. I'd pulled my blankets over my head to block the sunlight, but still heard him climbing the stairs and the particular creak that meant he was walking toward my room. He knocked on the door as he opened it. "*What?*" I said.

"Come on a bike ride with me?" he said.

I stuck my head out from the covers. "Now?"

"Well, after breakfast."

"Where?"

"Hound's Run."

A subdivision across the street from my elementary school, Hound's Run had given me my first experience with losing place. In third grade, my classmates and I stood on the school playground and watched bulldozers roll into the woods we'd treasured. The next summer, a group of us carried out a sort of junior eco-terrorism campaign. We regularly crossed over the ridge from my friend's house, yanked all the plastic ties off the trees, tied them to rocks, and threw the rocks off the hillside. We believed, as children do, in the finality of our actions. If no one knew which trees to cut, they would all be left to grow.

The houses went up anyway. I hated Hound's Run.

"*Why* would I want to go there?" I whined, collapsing dramatically onto my pillows.

"Apples."

"*Apples?*"

"Yes, apples. A guy on the planning commission told me there are some lots way back in Hound's Run with orchards on them. But they're going to level them soon for houses. Someone should pick that last crop of apples."

After breakfast, I emptied the books from my knapsack and Dad and I rode over to Hound's Run. It was a steep climb up the ridge. The road was new and black with house numbers painted on the curbs. The houses, most of them brown brick with arched windows revealing high foyers, towered over us as we struggled up the hills. I knew that there were odd things about these houses because we had, as a family, explored one while it was under construction. Sure it was trespassing, but we'd figured we had a right to know what was being built on the field where we used to gather daffodils every spring. Inside the house, there was two of everything. Two staircases, two rooms that resembled dens, two distinct wings of the house. We realized that one was the children's wing. "These are all going to be houses for rich people who want to have kids without spending any time with them," my mother had growled.

The orchard was set in a basin between two ridges. The leaves were changing. The sky above us was deep and blue. Dad and I were the only people out there. We waded through thigh-high grass and chose our apples. I was surprised to find an apple orchard in the middle of the city. We'd always driven out to the country to pick fruit. Dad explained that this had been countryside once with orchards all over the place. This one might have belonged to the man who'd lived in our house in the early 1900s.

The apples were small and tart. I filled my backpack and the basket on my bicycle. Dad lashed a couple of tote bags into the child seat he'd never bothered to take off his 1970 Schwinn. We spent the afternoon in the kitchen with my mother, listening to Brubeck and slicing apples. Because of the angle of the sun, autumn was the only time of year that the floors in our house felt warm. Sunlight flooded in. The breeze carried the smell of burning leaves and the sounds of construction work in the valley. Mom and Dad danced a little. I felt sad that we'd only discovered the orchard just before it would be destroyed. "But at least you found it," said my mother. "You gave it one last harvest."

Perhaps all you can really have of a place are the things you carry from it—like my memories of jazz, dishes clanging in the sink, and a crooked floor that felt solid enough for me. But perhaps the place holds onto you as well. Wood is, after all, cut from a living thing. It is porous, requires food and water. It shifts and moves. It absorbed us as we breathed it in.

Autumn now in West Virginia and the weather is warm and breezy. From my kitchen table, I can see that the maple outside my kitchen has gone yellow. I have my window open and some leaves and seeds occasionally skitter across the linoleum. Dad has called again with some interesting news. The handyman they hired to fix the plumbing won't work in our old house at night any more. It seems he kept hearing footsteps going up and down the stairs, even though he was all alone. I am excited by this news, instantly transported back to those nights when I believed I heard the moonshiners behind my wall.

"Wow! I always thought that place might be haunted!" I said. "Didn't you?"

The line grew silent and I knew he was thinking.

"No," he said. "If any spirits are haunting that house, they're ours."

# THAT'S WHAT WE'RE DOING HERE

### HIGHWAY 16, MAY 2004

"You checked their *mail?*" Rosanne asks. Her face registers surprise—or is it disgust? She's driving, south of Moorcroft, Wyoming, and I can only see her profile. We talk over the wind. The Subaru doesn't climb hills well with the air conditioner on. I realize I've offended her, but I continue my story.

"Yeah, it's the best way to get a name spelled right and all. Then you can start figuring out the connections—if they were related to anybody important, that kind of stuff."

Rosanne's features harden. The wind blows her hair away from her olive-skinned face and I can see plainly that her mouth is a thin line. Her dark eyes, throwing sparks, are focused on the asphalt, on the next gentle rise of the prairie as straight and true as the last. "Great, Erin. Raiding victims' mail. Nice."

She downshifts. The car lurches slightly. Neither of us speaks. I turn up the U2 mix, fingering the camera on my lap, and turn my face away from her, pretending to search the horizon for a good prairie shot. Really, I'm hiding my embarrassment. My face has always been too easy to read.

I rarely tell stories about my life as a newspaper reporter, but when I do, I tailor them to my audience. People like Rosanne prefer the ones where I helped re-open a homeless shelter or accosted the Governor about public education cuts during a photo op. They do not need, or want, to know that I stalked the perimeter of crime scenes and sorted through the mail of people who were still cooling under a sheet in the yard. They do not need, or want, to know that whenever someone had died doing something particularly stupid, a reporter could be counted on to walk around the newsroom hawking the story satirically: "Darwin's theory proved, A-3."

Having told Rosanne the wrong story, there's nothing I can do but watch the hills and the racing shadow of the Subaru as it carries us toward South Dakota. I can't sort it all out and put it back into a steel box. I can't follow a line, or the rule of thirds, and contain it all in an artful shot. Guilty, I still want to brag.

## THE PICAYUNE ITEM, MISSISSIPPI, MAY 1998

My first reporting job was a college internship in Picayune, Mississippi, about an hour from New Orleans. I turned 20 on my last day of work there. A blue highway sign at the top of the exit ramp into town proclaimed "Jesus is Lord Over Picayune." Like many small Southern cities, it was straight, flat, and sun-baked, split physically and mentally between gentility and a hardscrabble struggle to survive. At *The Picayune Item*, I answered to three employees, but I stuck closest to John, the city reporter. John wore his hair in a style reminiscent of the Blue Oyster Cult and was constantly pushing wild bangs off his forehead while he typed. His preferred gait was the bound. He took a delight in the work of a reporter that I have never seen equaled by anyone in any field since. Every assignment was a mission, and he leapt into it without looking back.

The *Item* had a brand-new color printing press that needed showing off, so it was my job to find front-page photographs. Every morning I roamed along the blazing white sidewalks shooting pictures of kids with lemonade stands, men working on cars, teenagers at the city pool, prize-winning garden flowers. A shot I took of Amtrak's Southern Crescent blurring past a historic Shay locomotive actually earned me some small-town fame. Between that and the Little League beat, I rarely had to show my ID when I wrote checks. It amazed me to see, all over town, something that I had framed in a viewfinder hugely magnified.

Most days by 10 a.m. it was too hot to be outside. I'd take my film to the Winn-Dixie and then return to the newsroom, where we suffered through human interest stories.

"Couldn't somebody rob a bank?" I asked. With its proximity to the interstate, Picayune's businesses were robbed on a regular basis. Crooks and dealers, apparently undeterred by Jesus' lordship, would hold up the Dollar Store or the Texaco and then flee to Louisiana. There had been a rash of bank and strong-arm robberies that spring.

"Hush!" said the county reporter. She was afraid to go to Winn-Dixie after dark or swim in creeks. "You don't want that, that was hell."

"That was better than this," John replied.

I agreed with John. I wanted to be on the scene of something rending and violent. I wondered about the air in such a place. Was it charged with adrenaline? Could you smell gunfire? If there was a death, did the air move in mortal resonance? Would I be able to capture that in newsprint and gelatin?

John kept his old journalism textbooks lined up on his desk, and I riffled through them during those slow news days. I always ended up at the same picture in *The Art of Journalism*. It captivated and horrified me at the time, and, later that summer, gave me comfort. John first showed it to me the morning after we'd argued over the ethical implications of hoping for a bank robbery.

The photograph is a black-and-white shot of a mother, father, and two young brothers. As I remember it, one brother lies on his back on the ground. His cheeks seem slightly swollen, and his eyes are large and dark, looking past his family into the sky. His lips are parted as if he has just exhaled. A paramedic is crouched over the boy's chest about to zip the bag over his face.

The older brother looks as if anguish has actually ratcheted him off the ground. He is straight as a pole, ribs sticking out. His elbows are tucked into his bare sides, his shoulders pulled up towards his ears; his face, turned upward, shows teeth clenched, and one hand covers his eyes. This brother is so far up on his tiptoes he's beginning to fall sideways. His mother has her arm around his waist just above his swimming trunks. She is steadying him while staring down at her dead son.

The photograph ran in *The Bakersfield Californian* during the summer of 1976. The textbook explains that the family had been swimming in a river where several people had already drowned that summer. The photographer had come back from the assignment with several shots that were not so graphic, but he and the editor both felt that it was important to run the one that captured grief and death most forcefully. Several people cancelled their subscriptions to the paper after the picture ran. But no one else drowned that summer.

"That's what we're doing here!" John had said to me, stabbing at the book with his index finger. "That's what reporting can do."

### HIGHWAY 16, MAY 2004

After a couple years, I gave up reporting and moved to Montana to work with AmeriCorps and write. Now I'm moving back east to teach. Rosanne has a couple weeks before she begins grassroots work campaigning for John Kerry, so this cross-country trek is her vacation.

When Rosanne graduated from college a few years ago, she and some classmates joined a movement vowing they would never take a job that compromised their morals or the greater good. They signed a contract promising that they would never act unethically or rely on the disclaimer, "Well, it's my job." Nine months into my reporting career at the time, I could have signed no such pact. This bothered me, but in journalism telling the truth trumps all other considerations.

And I really was bold. Once, I leaned over the crime tape and began reading notes off a clipboard an officer had left on the hood of his cruiser. I didn't know anyone had noticed until the clipboard disappeared. In the stories I tell, I stared up at Columbia's chief detective impassively, even impudently. Actually, I remember setting my jaw to hide the fear that must have shot briefly through my eyes when he yelled. I remember it was dusk and he blended with the dark as he towered over me. His name was Captain Messick and he usually called me "honey." As I nervously typed out the story later that night, Messick called and apologized for "hollering like that." He said he would have to be careful with his notes around a reporter who had so much "pluck and gumption."

I remember my stories and become that person again, willing to tell the truth at any cost. I have nothing to be ashamed of, no reason to sit in silence as the car rolls along. In my mind I say to Rosanne, "Listen, chick. I know you work for non-profits and get to save the world every day. But you read the paper over breakfast. You think those *Washington Post* reporters got where they are by being polite? They did the same as me. Spare me the self-righteous crap." I don't say this out loud. It's mean. I don't know if I like my side of the argument, anyway.

A fence line cuts an angle from the horizon and I freeze the flowing prairie with my camera. But it keeps moving. We keep moving. I know the edges of my shot will be blurred.

*THE DAILY HERALD,*
COLUMBIA, TENNESSEE, JANUARY 2001

Reporters uncovering a story claim to hope that nothing catastrophic has occurred—no foul play or crippling tragedies—but a secret, guilty desire for such a monumental event often wells inside them. Working the swing shift at a paper 40 miles south of Nashville, I became proficient at gathering images, putting them together quickly, figuring out connections. Some of those images became photographs that made it onto a page, others are framed only in my consciousness; all of them tell stories I didn't finish.

One sharp January afternoon I stood at the end of a mile-long gravel drive and stared up at a brick plantation house. Someone had found a body in the yard. At least, that's what we believed. The cops were saying very little across the scanner. I took my camera and went out with another reporter, Sarah, to wait, on a perfect Middle Tennessee winter day. The sky was brilliant and deep, contrasting sharply with the tall dead grass that lined both sides of the gravel drive and covered the hillside. The trees rose sharply, black lines rising out of the yellow, piercing the blue.

This image, the yellow and black and blue, is so luminous in my mind that I squint when I recall it. The one that we ran in the paper the next day shows a cruiser coming down the drive and the stately house at the upper left corner of the frame. In the picture, you can see people in the yard, but not the crime tape.

After Sarah and I had waited a while, I decided to walk to the three houses in sight and ask the neighbors if they had seen or heard anything. The woman in the antebellum home next door told me she'd had no idea anything was going on at all until I told her. No one was home in the white frame houses across the highway. I checked the mailboxes and wrote down the names for later.

We finally got the body's name that evening, long after we'd left the scene. It was a 19-year-old black kid named Shawn Williams. He had an arrest record, mostly drugs and thefts, and his family's address appeared at the top of his rap sheet. My editor told me to drive out to the family's house to get a statement from the parents and a decent picture of the victim. Sarah stayed by the phone and waited for Messick to call. A sheriff's deputy had told her that an arrest was imminent. We were going to run Shawn's criminal record in the paper. The crime was probably not random.

The Williams' neighborhood was crammed with cars and people

milling around the street outside their house. I parked half a block away, and ducked through a crowd of teenage girls to get to the gate. They glared at me; I stared at my shoes. The yard was filled with darkened Christmas decorations, but a light was on in every room in the house.

Someone inside had seen me coming up the path and the door opened before I knocked. A woman blocked the light with her enormous frame, her arms folded across her chest.

"And what do *you* want?" she said.

"Who is it?" another voice called out.

"It's a damn reporter," the woman said.

"Come in! Let her in!"

The woman stepped out of the way to reveal a comfortable, square room filled with flowers and framed photographs. I could smell pasta cooking. On the couch, two old people slumped, looking like they would not be eating. They were Shawn's parents, haggard and beaten by news only a few hours old.

"You want to know about Shawn?" the father said. He was clean-shaven and wore a tan jacket over a sweater. The house was very warm.

"Yes, yes sir. I'm with *The Daily Herald*. I'm sorry for your loss; I want to know how…well, how you feel." It was such a stupid question and the one I always came up with when I interviewed mourners. Usually at this point a family member would tell me to fuck off, and I'd return to the office and write "so-and-so's family did not wish to comment."

Shawn's mother left the room. The father invited me to sit down.

"How I feel," he said in a Tennessee baritone. "Well, how I feel is this. In a few days, I will bury my only son. No father should ever have to bury his only son. No parents should outlive their children—and I do not understand—I just do not understand why this had to happen."

If I hadn't been working, I would have put my arm on Mr. Williams' shoulder, asked if I could do anything, agreed that the death was beyond comprehension, promised to make them a casserole. Instead, I wrote down what he said.

The mother returned with a photo album in her hand. She cleared space on the coffee table, laid it out in front of me. Here was a child in his church clothes: Shawn. There was Shawn playing basketball, Shawn going to a prom. I asked if there was a picture we could print and she produced a wallet-sized senior photo. "Olan Mills 2000" was embossed in a bottom corner. She told me about his interests, that he had always gone to church. The father chimed in. I think he must have read my face because he told me that he and his wife had known things were going wrong for Shawn. They'd thought they had more time. He was a good kid.

I realized as they spoke that Shawn's parents would be looking for a eulogy in the morning paper. I could feel the color rising in my cheeks. I wrote down everything they said, staring hard at the yellow lined paper. I slipped the photo between the pages and the back cover of my notebook and promised to return it to them the following evening. They thanked me for coming and walked me to the door, repeating that he was just a kid, a good kid. He hadn't deserved such an ending. They thought they had more time.

There had been an arrest. "A man and a woman. I have the mug shots," Sarah told me when I walked into the newsroom. She showed me two pictures on computer paper. The man was hard and lean with a prominent jaw. The woman had long, stringy hair. She was clowning around in the mug shot, turning her head at an angle, sticking out her tongue, puffing her cheeks, crossing her eyes. I wished her dead.

They were friends of Shawn's, but he'd owed them drug money. So they'd picked him up and drove around, buying fast food and killing time. Around one a.m., they pulled up the driveway of an antebellum home, probably thinking it was a long country road. I wondered if Shawn had gotten nervous at this point; I wondered what they'd told him. Somehow they got him out of the car, near an outbuilding. Then they pistol-whipped him, put a silencer on the gun, and shot him once in the back of the head.

I had to write the truth, of course. So I typed up Shawn's arrest record, wrote a couple of lines about his love of music and basketball, and added what his father had said about burying him. The next evening, I stopped at an Albertson's and bought a pink tulip. I held it with two fingers away from the steering wheel as I drove back to the Williams house. As soon as the mother opened the door, I could see she felt betrayed. There were dark circles under her eyes. She did not speak. I was taller than she was and could see over her head into the living room where I'd sat the night before. I'd bought the flower believing she would accept it as a small but sincere gesture. It would be a sign that their tragedy had touched people who see tragedy on a regular basis. But then, looking into a room filled with elaborate floral arrangements, piles of cards, and dishes covered in foil, I realized how she would see it. A single grocery-store flower: the cheap gesture of a reporter trying to assuage her guilt. All this was evident in the light from the doorway. I held it out to her with the senior portrait. She took them, spit a thank you, and slammed the door. I walked through the yard among the darkened hulks of plastic snowmen and toy soldiers. The teenagers were at the gate again. I caught their look, clenched my teeth, and shot it back a little harder.

The Williams' neighborhood was on a ridgetop. From my car, I could see all the lights of the city framed by winter trees. Columbia itself was massive and bright. Lights rimmed the outlying highways, including the one near where Shawn was killed. I could also see the Waffle House where I often stopped for vanilla Cokes after work if I'd nailed a particularly good story. And I knew that I had written a good story about Shawn, the right story. But I didn't feel like celebrating. I sat in the car with my anger and guilt and sadness, trying to figure out where one ended and the other began. Self-justification was in the mix too, probably with the anger. The lights blurred and suddenly I was weeping for all of those things. It didn't take long. I leaned my forehead on the steering wheel, four or five sobs and I was done. I never cried again, over any story. And I never went back to the Waffle House. That night, I started the car, wiped my cheeks with the heel of my hand, and drove back to work.

### HIGHWAY 16, MAY 2004

The story I was telling Rosanne is hanging out in space, unfinished. I like to end my stories with a joke or something to indicate that I'm not taking myself very seriously—even if I am. But if I speak now, I'll have to justify myself. I'm content to watch Wyoming and listen to Bono.

The first part of our trip took us through Glacier, Yellowstone, and the Grand Tetons. Amidst the jagged peaks, I was dreading the plains, but I've found they possess their own beauty. Space and shape resonate here. Already I've taken pictures of a pyramid of hay bales, a fence line, an "S" shaped creek mimicking the horizon's rolling hills. The shapes stand out because of the distance between them. Even a weather-beaten telephone pole is worth noting, because it's in a line with 50 identical poles stretching to the horizon. It's easy to see patterns, easy to create them in the viewfinder, even in a moving car. There are no mysteries, no contexts to consider, and no consequences when my camera reveals the truth and shape of things. I cannot take my eyes off the prairie because I'm afraid I might miss something.

## TENNESSEE, AUGUST 2001

People say that jokes are a coping mechanism for employees in high-stress jobs, but that's only a partial truth. What jokes do is make you better than their subjects—jokes create distance. You can frame a dead person into a space you will not occupy. The problem is, such distance cannot be contained to an eight-hour shift. Eventually, everyone deserves his fate but you.

I covered two drownings the summer after Shawn was killed and they did not fall into my idea of a mission. The second drowning occurred on a Saturday that had already been busy and chaotic. By the time the call came across the scanner, the man had already been given up for dead.

"Yeah, we're going to need the boat out at the quarry. A man dove in headfirst. Looks like there may be alcohol involved," said the voice on the scanner.

Kevin, the weekend editor, looked at me.

"Oh come *on*, Kevin! Wouldn't my time be better spent writing a public service announcement? Notice to Maury County Residents—you do not have gills." I punched the headline in the air with my hands.

"Be sure you're back in plenty of time to write that up," Kevin said.

"How is this even *news*? If one of these dumbasses stayed *afloat*, now *that* would be news," I said.

"No shit," William, the copy editor, added.

"Take the camera," Kevin said.

"And bring us back a beer if there's any left," William said.

We laughed.

It was sunset when I got to the quarries. An ambulance was pulling away, its lights off. I had learned long ago what that signified.

I approached the young detective on the scene, who told me he had to ask the man's wife some questions, but then he would answer mine. He pointed to where they'd found the body and I wandered over to the spot.

There was an open cooler with some cans of Bud Light floating in ice water. A striped blue towel was draped over a boulder. I could see shelves of rock through the water below. There wasn't much to photograph, but I framed a shot of the rocky water and the cooler. It said enough. When I turned around, I could see the wife looking at me. She was middle-aged, scrawny and had a fake tan and peroxide hair.

The detective confirmed my suppositions. The wife had seen her husband strike his head before he disappeared into the murky green. Yet another drunken idiot.

This would earn a "Darwin's theory proved" in the newsroom. I went back up the trail without approaching the wife. I'd already written most of the article in my head and figured it would get about five inches. I was cutting through the weeds between two quarries when a car pulled up and a young woman about my age jumped out. She was a fat version of her mother, wearing a Tweety Bird shirt. She looked right past me and came lumbering down the trail. I stepped aside.

"Is it Daddy?" she said, but she already knew, and she answered her own question. "It's Daddy, isn't it? It's Daddy. Oh, God."

There was resignation in her voice. I could tell that this ending did not surprise her. My throat tightened. She embraced her mother. I remembered John and *The Art of Journalism* and reached back for my camera. It was zipped into its bag and my fingertips collided with the metal teeth.

"Dammit!" I whispered. Still, I moved pretty fast, unzipping the bag and putting my hands on the camera in one motion. All I needed was for them to cry or hug about five more seconds. The older lady opened her eyes when I jerked the camera halfway out of the bag. We looked at each other. She broke the embrace and said something to her daughter. Then she pointed at me. The daughter flipped me the bird, and they walked away. I took a picture of their backs.

## HIGHWAY 16, MAY 2004

I can't tell if Rosanne is still angry or just lost in thought. We're heading for the Black Hills. We'll sleep in the Badlands tonight. We read all about them in a *National Geographic* yesterday.

I left my job and moved to Montana when I realized I couldn't separate myself into two people. There are reporters who can. But once I began to shape my world into one-liners at The Daily Herald, it bled over into my private life. Right and wrong moved into soft focus. I was tied up in pursuing the truth, but how much really gets revealed in 20 inches of newsprint? I compressed entire lives into something that would fit into two days' coverage, and then I left them. Outside of work, I was not even writing stories, just reducing people to caricatures.

My father gave me a photography book when I was a teenager, black and white shots of steam trains. Inside the cover he wrote, "Whatever you do with your life, don't do it just for truth and beauty. Do it for God and then for others and then for yourself." In Montana, I worked with troubled youth. We planted a community garden and I moved past truth and beauty. At the newspapers, I knew that people's lives deserved more attention as surely as I knew I needed to start my stories with the inverted pyramid. But there wasn't space and I no longer cared.

Even now, I have no intention of apologizing to Rosanne or admitting any lack of moral judgement. I am proud of what I did, and that is what frightens me.

## MISSISSIPPI 1998

Having finished my morning photo search, I was hammering out an article previewing the Poplarville Blueberry Jubilee when a scream came over the scanner. It ended before I realized I'd heard it. A loud beep followed and then a cop called for assistance with a signal two. I stumbled around, trying to make it over to the code sheet to see what a "signal two" meant, but John already knew. He was hitting save on his computer and grabbing his keys and notebook all in one motion. "That's a shooting," he said, as he hustled past the editor.

"Erin, go with him. Take a camera," the editor said.

I tried to move quickly, but John was already framed by sunlight and a closing door before I could save my work and pick up a notebook. Not wanting to waste time in the camera room, I yanked John's giant Minolta off his desk as I ran past, cradled it to my chest, and met him in the parking lot.

Shootings were extremely rare in Picayune. A man from advertising named Joey drove us to the scene as an excuse to see the action. We raced across town in his Beretta. An ambulance was pulling away as we approached the scene. Its lights were off and it was in no hurry, which John said means either everything or nothing. There was a line of cruisers parked on the street and a formidable portion of two yards were encircled in yellow crime tape. John waved to a cop as we drove past and he pointed down the street. "Y'all wait back there, someone'll fill you in," the officer said.

So we parked a little way down the street and began waiting, squinting to see the action at 1204 Washington Street.

A couple of familiar-looking boys biked by while we languished around the car. Beads of sweat glistened on their dark foreheads. Their tires left little diamond-shaped prints in the heat-softened tar. The smaller one, who looked to be about nine, turned, biked very close, and looked up at me. "Hey!" he said, squinting. "You're the picture lady! You put my picture in the paper Sunday."

It took me a second to recognize the kid without his pine green uniform and green socks pulled up past his knees. "You're Nicholas Christmas," I said. The kid was obviously thrilled that I remembered his name, but who could forget a name like that? His friend, older, sat back from us a bit. His name was Avery McDonald, and he'd been on the front page, too. I could hardly believe these were the same kids—or that they had lives beyond the perfect realm of the baseball diamond at Friendship Park.

"Are you going to take our picture again?" asked Nicholas. "Take it again! Take it again!"

I told him I couldn't because I needed the film for another story. He frowned and whined, then backed his bike away. "Hey!" I said. "You guys played a great game on Friday. You almost won."

"Yeah, we did!"

"Maybe you'll beat 'em next year."

"Yeah!" Nicholas had the coolest grin I'd ever seen.

"See you around."

"See ya, picture lady!" They stood up on their pedals to pass the house and disappeared beyond the squad cars.

John and Joey and I were alone again, waiting for the cops to feed us the story. Joey, with his short-cropped hair and bright polo shirt, was the only one of us who didn't look wilted. I peeled off my linen blazer and set it on the roof of the car. John rolled up the sleeves of his yellow oxford and loosened his tie. Sweat made his hair droop over his eyes; he occasionally swiped it away with one hand, shielded his eyes from the sun, and tried to see what was happening at the house.

The three of us leaned against the trunk and watched the cops watch us. We all looked like cardboard cutouts. John and Joey puffed endlessly on Marlboro Lights. I danced from foot to foot because I wanted to do something. We knew the police wouldn't talk until they were ready.

Another squad car drove by, not the chief, but someone else with rank. John and Joey recognized him. A beat officer strode gravely down to meet him. He turned to us, shaking his head. "It's real bad in there," he said.

"What? What?" We practically leapt toward him.

"A death."

"How? Who?"

"There'll be a press release later today." The cops walked back up the driveway, toward the side door.

I scuffed some loose gravel. It didn't look like we were going to get any news. We didn't even know who was dead. I stood there, bombarded by the heat, the cigarette haze encasing the Beretta, and felt my sense of reality falter: The events up the street seemed like they were happening on a movie screen. We were about to leave when another car pulled up, a silver Ford Taurus. A heavyset woman wearing a pink shirt and tight grey pants lunged out, wailing incoherently. She approached the yard at 1204. I tried to believe I was watching a nightly news recap.

I heard a voice say, "You need to go get that." I felt like a third-grader forgetting her line in the school play. My right hand supported the camera lens, a sweaty hunk of metal and glass. I stared blankly at John and Joey. "This is you," John's drawling voice was soft but assertive, "Get it, Scoop."

I stepped forward, a hand pushing me from behind, between my shoulder blades. After five steps I planted my feet, brought the Minolta to my eye, and zoomed the lens all the way, remembering to steady the camera body with my palm. The woman, flailing her arms, screamed, "Please tell me she's all right. Please tell me she's all right." Click. A man, her brother I guessed, approached her, wrapped his thin arms around her shoulders. I took two more steps. Steady. Click. The brother let her go, looked her in the eyes and muttered something. Three more steps. Click. Now the woman knew the truth. It crashed down on her, knocked her to her knees and I fell with her. Click. Click.

Ms. Leola Jordan, 91 years old, a member of Weems Chapel United Methodist Church and great-great grandmother of two, had been murdered—not shot, but stabbed multiple times in the middle of the night. Nobody knew why.

### HIGHWAY 16, MAY 2004

I realize that my story has upset Rosanne because it reveals a part of myself I've kept hidden from her. On this road trip, we've listened primarily to U2, Ladysmith Black Mambazo, and the Indigo Girls. We've talked about social justice and politics—topics emphasizing the value of human life. This is all part of who I am, but so is the reporting. I was a good reporter. I wrote well; I exposed the truth, I was bold. I'm not sorry.

Of course, Rosanne really doesn't want an apology. Likely she's as confused about the incongruities in my life as I am. In any case, the need for silence passes. We cross the border into South Dakota.

"What is South Dakota?" Rosanne asks.

I grab our atlas and flip it open.

"Well, I think with the Badlands, it should be *The Bad-Ass State*, but apparently it's *The Land of Rushmore*. Did you know there's a new book out about the history of Rushmore? It's crazy."

"No. What's it say?" Rosanne asks.

The conversation flows as surely as prairie grass in the wind.

Rosanne and I have been friends since we worked together at a nonprofit one summer. We ran an emergency home-repair project, and I knew then as I know now that she is one of those people who inspires compassion by demonstrating it. On this trip, we have listened to the life stories of highway workers, park rangers, and gas station attendants. When I'm around Rosanne, I'm reminded that I exist in a world of stories, that I don't want to distance myself from people. I also realize how often I still shape and reduce and sequester myself from the stories that continue all around me. I wonder if that will ever change.

## WASHINGTON STREET, MISSISSIPPI 1998

When we returned to 1204 Washington Street, neighbors and family saw me coming with the giant Minolta, and they signaled each other and turned their backs. I wanted to reach over to their shoulders, to cry and apologize, but instead I let the shutter open and close over the crime tape, over relatives weeping softly into bunched up Kleenex, over the victim's laundry still hanging on the line. The film was developed at the Winn-Dixie and around 5:00 p.m. John ran into the newsroom: "I think you may have really nailed a shot." He handed me the negative and I held it up to the florescent light and saw Miss Leola's daughter dropping to her knees, her brother holding one of her elbows as she fell. I exhaled violently. I felt proud and evil. The picture ran on the front page of the next day's paper.

# OUR MOST SEGREGATED HOUR

*For as the body apart from the spirit is dead,
so faith apart from works is dead.*
—Book of James 2:26

### WE WALK BY FAITH, NOT BY SIGHT, 2006

Three days after Christmas, after the realtor had pulled the SOLD sign from the front yard, after I'd helped my parents load the last piece of furniture into the U-haul, I paced the front yard and empty rooms of my childhood home, wondering if any place would ever again seem as familiar to me. In the moment's sadness, I had forgotten where I would be on New Year's morning, the place I always go to on my increasingly rare Sundays in Nashville. Four days later, I swung my rented Ford into a parking space and rushed up the sidewalk, past the magnolia tree, up the stone stairs, and through the high, white doorway. The choir sang the Introit as my footsteps echoed up the stairway to the balcony. At the top, the sanctuary of Calvary United Methodist Church stretched before me. Actually being inside the sanctuary and gazing out over the rows of pews is like adding color to an artist's sketch; for that church is one of those places I'm always seeing somewhere deep inside myself.

Winter sunlight was just hitting the arched windows along the southern exposure, drawing lines across the cream walls, the white pews with wood trim and red cushions. Atop the altar there's a brass cross, the elements for communion covered in white linen, and six candles. Behind the choir there's another high, arched window, with the outline of a cross sparkling in the glass. According to the Christian calendar it was still Christmas, so everything that Sunday was white: the ministers' robes, the choir's stoles, the fringed cloth hanging from the lectern. It was obvious to me on that vivid January morning that whoever designed the sanctuary over 50 years ago meant for it to be resplendent. But it also feels close and familiar to me. Even with my life and church in another town, I fall easily into the rhythm of worship at Calvary, knowing many of the songs, creeds, and prayers by heart. I dream during the organ music. I try to focus during the sermon and prayers.

Because I am white, it almost goes without saying that most of the rest of the congregation is, too. Martin Luther King, Jr. often said that 11:00 a.m. Sunday was "the most segregated hour in Christian America." In the Nashville of the '80s and '90s, I was going to school with black children. I was learning about the evils of segregation and heroes of the Civil Rights Movement at both church and school, but Calvary, the place I loved most, was as white as it had been in the late '50s, when King was leading Ebenezer Baptist in Atlanta, and Sam Dodson was in Calvary's pulpit 180 miles north.

The redoubt from a Civil War skirmish is intact on the Calvary grounds, right between the parking lot and the preschool. A stone wall that slaves built to mark a plantation boundary now separates the property from the four-lane chaos of Hillsboro Road. When I was in children's choir, we learned about spirituals and sang, "Swing Low, Sweet Chariot." The slave wall was visible from the choir room window, just past the spot of green where we had our yearly Easter egg roll. I tried to picture gnarled slave hands laying rock on rock, then bullets whizzing past the wall while soldiers crested the hill that now is a parking lot. But at six years old, it was hard for me to believe anything except Calvary had ever existed in that space, much less that musket balls had split the air where our sanctuary stands today. Of course, church sanctuaries are just that—existing to provide an hour apart from those battles and trenches in which we are so often enmeshed. They're designed to give some space for contemplation so that worshippers, when they step back into the world, can live and act according to their religion's teachings. Faith—all the goodness and decency and action taught at 10:30 worship—should never be sequestered within those high white walls. Making sure it's not is a weekly struggle.

On that New Year's Day, after the last hymn had been sung and the acolyte had extinguished the candles, the emptying room filled with the aroma of warm wax and smoke. I will forever associate that smell with contentment—catching up with friends among the pews for a few minutes after the service, knowing that Sunday dinner awaits. The most common farewell after worship at Calvary is, "Have a good week." People raise their arms in a broad wave, calling to each other across the parking lot. Have a good week. Like a mother telling her child to have a good day at school—go out and be in the world, do well, and then return home.

## PROPHET IN HIS OWN LAND, 1958

*Somewhere somebody must have some sense.*
—Martin Luther King, Jr.

In the summer of 1958, a quarter century before I first stepped into the sanctuary at Calvary clutching my mother's hand, Sam Dodson, Jr., a 42-year-old preacher with a buzz cut and thick glasses, stood in the pulpit at Calvary and looked over the congregation for the first time. This new minister had spent his boyhood on a farm in a hamlet about 60 miles south of Nashville, boarded with friends while attending high school in town (he graduated from Hume-Fogg, like me), and went on to college at Vanderbilt. This is, so far, the perfect pedigree for a Nashville preacher—born in a small town, but experienced with the big city, like many of his parishioners. Sam had gone on to Yale Divinity School and led some churches in New York, then returned to the South and worked in counties surrounding Nashville before Calvary, his first big appointment.

New-minister Sundays are always awkwardly electric. It's an abrupt transition from a minister who has led the church for years to a complete stranger. Even though I wasn't there, I can picture the moment when Sam took the pulpit. Perhaps he sipped from a glass of water while every congregant waited for the first words from his lips. The previous minister, Willard Blue, had been responsible for an unprecedented growth in membership. The sanctuary had been built during his tenure, and it probably still glistened with newness as Sam gazed over the sea of faces. People who were there that morning remember that Sam told a story about growing up on a farm in the South to begin his sermon. When he was a boy, he'd said, he and the other white boys chucked rocks at the black kids in town.

How did the congregation react to this revelation, I wonder? Even in the segregated Nashville of the late 1950s, such violence was considered lowbrow—carried out only by hicks and toughs. Nashville was not Birmingham or Jackson, but the entrenched kingdom of the white moderate. The city had black policemen and councilmen, even a black reporter at the conservative *Nashville Banner's* news desk. Most white Nashvillians prided themselves on their "progressive" approach to race issues. Did the members of Calvary that morning, so many of them from small Southern towns, recall similar experiences from their own childhoods? Were they appalled? It's most likely they sensed that the sermon they were about to hear could not be discussed in conversations over pot roast that afternoon. In Nashville's white community, polite people did not, and do not, discuss race isssues.

But Sam continued with his sermon. He told his new flock that he'd repented many times for the hateful acts he'd committed as a boy. Now that he was back in Nashville, a city where the Civil Rights Movement was building substantial momentum, he planned on doing everything he could to challenge segregation. Taking action against injustice was, he explained, mandated by Christian teachings.

The buzz that would crescendo into a roar in five years began that very afternoon. Some members were afraid that a minister taking such a strong stance might split the church, and some feared blacks would come to worship in their new sanctuary. "They were just scared to death," Sam's widow, Helen, told me over the phone. After church on that pleasant June Sunday in 1958, some members threatened to walk out if Sam ever again preached desegregation. Others supported him. Most tended to the business of their daily lives and waited for the storm to pass.

It did pass eventually, but not without carving its own deep lines in the church's mental landscape. Through it all, Sam remained unflappable in his conviction that Calvary members, mostly powerful whites, needed to be held accountable for their actions, their ethics, and the faith they claimed to possess.

## WHEN I WAS A CHILD, I THOUGHT LIKE A CHILD, 1987

I remember the first quivering moment in that church when I realized that the words of a sermon might apply to me. I was about nine years old, staring up at the pulpit of the Rev. Dr. Jim Beasley, a grandfatherly intellectual who had silver, square-rimmed glasses, a shock of dark grey hair, and a rasp in his voice from the cigarettes he smoked behind the church offices. After I'd received the customary third-graders' Bible, with my full name embossed in gold on its fake leather cover, my parents expected me to stop drawing my weekly comic strip about talking ponies when the sermon began. I learned, years later, that Dr. Beasley is considered the most erudite preacher Calvary's ever had. He's also the only minister I've ever addressed by anything other than his first name. It's not that he wasn't kind. He often took parishioner's families fishing with his own family. One Christmas, my friend Brandon and I helped him and his son harvest greenery from their farm for the sanctuary wreaths. But something about Dr. Beasley's gravity in the pulpit, his scholarly air, dictated that no child or teenager ever considered calling him "Jim."

Dr. Beasley liked to punctuate his preaching with questions from scripture. *Does this sound like you? Are you truly the Samaritan who stops, or are you the priest who doesn't have enough time?* I can't remember the exact question he posed when I realized I hadn't been acting as I should, only that it involved having " a pure heart," and that I remembered my latest fight with Charlotte. We were friends, Charlotte and I, but I thought she was bossy, and worse, a goody two-shoes. She thought I was a rule-breaking smart-ass, an impression I cultivated just to torment her. Whenever I made her angry, she'd put her hands on her hips and say, "Go suck an egg!"

"Charlotte doesn't count," I remember thinking. "God knows she's bossy and I don't have to be nice to her." But I did, and in that question about a pure heart, I knew I'd failed. I felt the same quaky dread I felt whenever I made my little sister cry, an instantaneous, complete panic. For me, punishment was not the issue so much as shame. I didn't mind being sent to my room, a room full of drawing paper and books. The sting of a spanking wore off.

Shame, however, left me alone with my conscience. Listening to a sermon in church that grapples with your specific sins can make you feel nothing *but* shame, nothing but your own silent acknowledgement of accountability. Dr. Beasley was not going to send me to my room. There would be no smiting, but I *had* disappointed a God who'd done nothing but love me.

I sank down in my pew, certain that the entire congregation could see shame swirling from my barrettes down to my penny loafers. Dr. Beasley's next words, whatever they were, moved me from shame to resolve. "Tomorrow, I won't be mean to her," I thought. I probably wasn't, but certainly fell back into the old pattern before long. That is our nature after all. There have been countless sermon epiphanies for me since that day nearly 20 years ago. That same uneasiness, the need to escape or deny, always rushes over me before I decide to take action.

### I REASONED AS A CHILD, 1990

Sam's sermons were concise, always about 10 minutes long, and in them he usually tied the morning's scripture to a call for action against injustice. He focused on segregation. Jim Crow was just beginning to loose its hold on Nashville, but not without a fight. In 1958, when Sam began preaching at Calvary, Nashville's public schools had just ended their first year as an integrated system, a year that began with a midnight bombing at a school where one black child had enrolled.

Also in 1958, a young black minister named James Lawson arrived in Nashville by bus and enrolled in classes at Vanderbilt Divinity School. He had been sent by Martin Luther King himself. In Nashville, Lawson joined forces with two powerful ministers in the black community—C.T. Vivian and Kelly Miller Smith. Lawson led workshops on nonviolence at Smith's church.

Their goal was to change everything about the segregated environment of Nashville. They began with department stores downtown, holding sit-ins at the lunch counters and boycotting stores that did not treat blacks fairly. By February 1960, most downtown shops in Nashville accepted black and white customers and the movement had spread across the South.

A month later, Lawson was expelled from Vanderbilt for partaking in the sit-ins. Sam joined Reverends Lawson, Vivian, and Smith, as well as other ministers and rabbis, to form a coalition of ministers working for social justice. They marched and worked to integrate grocery stores, restaurants, and movie theatres; and every Sunday morning Sam preached at Calvary. Yet before I began researching my church's role in the movement, I'd never even heard his name.

Calvary has an Anderson Chapel, a Willard Blue Library, and a Masters Common. There's no Dodson anything. While combing through filing cabinets in the church archives one evening, I found a paragraph clipped from the church newsletter announcing that a small table in the sanctuary, where the empty offering plates are stacked every week, had been dedicated to him. Even our current head pastor, Peter, didn't know about the table. I've realized that churches, as a whole, are often not very focused on their histories, although many of them have a generational presence (at Calvary there are always pews filled with three or four generations of the same family, all of them lifelong members). This lack of historical perspective may exist because churches are always looking forward. There's always the next Sunday School lesson to plan, an upcoming senior luncheon, a new topic in Bible Study, all of it forever in the future.

Growing up, all the history I knew at Calvary was centered around physical artifacts. The Battle of Nashville, which was the last major Confederate offensive of the Civil War, is recalled by the vine-covered gulley that remains on church grounds. The church's first members met in the cafeteria at my middle school just a few weeks after Pearl Harbor was bombed. And just south of Calvary, on Hillsboro Road, there is another church whose founding Sam was, in a sense, responsible for. My family and I passed that church every Sunday. Calvary is a red brick building with a tarnished copper roof. The church we passed is white brick, with a towering white steeple and sanctuary doors and windows designed in the same style as Calvary's. This other church faced east, so it fairly shone when we passed it in the mornings—beautiful. One morning when I was about 10, I noticed its name—St. Paul Southern Methodist. "Hey!" I said, leaning my head over the front seats. "If we live in the South, why don't we go *there?*"

Mom scoffed. "You don't wanna go there."

"Why not?"

"The people who founded that church left Calvary. Our minister was in favor of integration and they didn't like it," Mom said.

"Isn't integration the good thing and segregation the bad thing?"

"Yes."

I was horrified that anyone would start a *church*, of all things, on a foundation of racial hatred, but mainly I was relieved that Calvary was on the right side of the issue. Like the Union soldiers' victory and the charter members who I always pictured meeting by candlelight during air raid drills, my church's history seemed to be dominated by the brave and the true. I was happy to be associated with the good guys.

There's really no need for metaphor about my innocence as a child. From age six to eighteen, I was literally a choirgirl. In middle school, I was an acolyte lighting candles, collecting offering plates, and assisting the ministers with a nervous solemnity. My friends and I were at church every Sunday morning and back in the evening for choir or youth group meetings. Then there were Wednesday Night Suppers with Sanctuary Choir rehearsals after that, where, as a high schooler, I learned Mozart, Bach, and Handel.

When I think of growing up at Calvary, I think of singing, and I think of constantly moving in a pack. I wish I could embody my entire childhood in a specific story—a story that could show how dissonant the notion of conflict and schism at Calvary seems to me. All I can think of, though, are Dylan Thomas' words about the Christmases he loved so well, that they so ran together he could not remember if it snowed for twelve days and twelve nights when he was six or six days and six nights when he was twelve. Calvary was like that, each week moving in its comfortable rhythm until the weeks became months, the seasons changed, the seasons became another year of Christmas greenery, Easter lilies, youth retreats, summer camps and harvest festivals; and it all began again. The children I grew up with there are still cherished friends, now expecting children of their own—more little heads in the family pews.

When we were young, my friends and I learned that God is love. We learned that this love compelled us to act, that faith without works is dead. We knew that. So we collected mittens at Christmas. We cooked meals for the homeless families who sheltered in the church gym once a week. We traveled out to Appalachia, repaired homes, loved the people, and learned about economic injustice. My friends and I did all of these things, but nobody took us into the church library to read the articles someone had clipped from *The Tennessean* and put in a manila envelope. No one told us that a former minister once fought to allow blacks to shop at the H.G. Hills Grocery Store down the street. The entire time I was at Calvary, nobody taught us about Sam.

## THE SPIRIT OF THE LORD, 1958-1963

Finding information about Sam's ministry and the events that led to St. Paul's founding was difficult. Sam has passed away, as have many of the more prominent St. Paul charter members—like the architect who designed Calvary's sanctuary and later drew up the plans for St. Paul's sanctuary, thus accounting for the similarities in style.

Forty-five years puts a gauzy haze over memory. Some of the oral histories I've gathered conflict with each other. What's more, many people who were around during those years insist that they don't know enough for me to interview them. They were busy, they've told me. Busy with work, busy raising children. They liked Sam and his sermons enough to stay, but laid low when "all that mess" with St. Paul began, just waited for it to end. One member told me, "I admired Sam's position; a lot of people did. But some didn't, and some of those people are the original founders of St. Paul. It was a time we had to live through, that's all." Every single person I've spoken with was glad I was researching Sam's story and trying to bring the truth to light. But although the pieces remain, the event has lost much of its immediacy in the minds of Calvary's parishioners.

In the early '80s, when memories of the schism were not quite so distant, my father was active in a church-based organization called Nashvillians in Favor of Nuclear Arms Freeze (NIFNAF). He offered Calvary's lawn for a NIFNAF ice cream social, a fundraiser. There was a localized yet passionate uproar in the church, and when my father went to the church Board for approval, it passed by only one vote. Dr. Beasley tried to persuade Dad to drop the issue entirely. "Jim said to me, 'You don't understand what happened here 20 years ago. It's very hard for this church to handle issues that are politically divisive.' Jim just felt that if the entire congregation sang from the same page of music, everyone would be a lot better off," Dad said. The ice cream social was a success, anyway. About 100 Methodists from four churches—West End, Belmont, Edgehill, and Calvary, gathered under the shade trees near the redoubt and talked about peace.

I've been told that Sam's time at Calvary has made it a more politically progressive church, a welcoming place for people like my parents—active in peace projects and anti-poverty campaigns. Other members say it's made everyone more respectful of beliefs across the spectrum. I wonder how my church can continue to navigate the line between being respectful and taking a stand. I don't know if the search for common ground within divisive issues is harmful or beneficial.

Sam's actual thoughts on the matter, the sermons he gave, are gone. There is only memory to carry us. Many former ministers from Calvary left their sermons in the church archives, spidery handwriting on lined sheets of notebook paper. Their files are voluminous. But Sam had a different ritual. Believing each congregation had specific spiritual needs, he burned his sermons whenever he moved so he wouldn't be tempted to reuse them. As a result, the manila folder devoted to Sam is quite thin. There are some newspaper articles, a brochure, an angry letter from a church committee and a response from the Board. There's a eulogy that ran in the church newsletter in 2002.

His widow, Helen, told me that Sam recognized that Calvary, a powerful, white church in the first large city where the modern Civil Rights Movement had a visible impact, required a call to action. Calvary members needed to know that scriptural calls for justice far outnumber those obscure few biblical passages that supremacists have used for centuries to justify segregation. When Sam preached, he was absolute, uncompromising. And when he was done, he tossed his words into the fire.

Jesus' first sermons, the ones he gave right after he'd hung up his carpentry tools, gotten baptized, and spent 40 days fasting in the wilderness, are also lost to time. The Gospel of Luke says only, "And he taught in their synagogues, being glorified by all." Luke did document, however, the first sermon Christ gave after he returned to his hometown. Jesus chose to share a text from Isaiah with his fellow Nazarenes. Luke reports that, "He opened the book and found the place where it is written, 'The Spirit of the Lord is upon me, because he has anointed me to preach good news to the poor. He has sent me to proclaim release to the captives and recovering of sight to the blind, to set at liberty those who are oppressed, to proclaim the acceptable year of the Lord.' And he said to them, 'Today, this scripture has been fulfilled in your hearing.'"

I once heard a minister speak about the significance of Jesus' choice. For Christians, he said, Jesus is not just a good man, but God made flesh, not just a leader but the very bedrock of faith; and the first documented scripture he chose to preach on was not about personal salvation, but a passage that actively encourages his followers to minister to the most downtrodden among them.

I liked that sermon so much I imitated it one summer when I had a job working with youth and repairing homes in the Appalachian Mountains. As a leader, I was responsible for evening programs to help the volunteers make connections between faith and works. To me, those verses from Luke were, still are, the embodiment of that connection. Tired, dirty, and sore from the day's labor, I'd step onto a rickety classroom chair each week and recite that sermon on Jesus' first message to a new group of volunteers. Among a crowd of community service-charged teenagers, I had a receptive audience. It seemed to me that no matter how poorly the day had gone, or how hopeless things seemed, those words were instructional, powerful, and true. I'd stand on that chair and let my voice gather and roll like a wave. Then, I'd close my Bible with a crack and listen to the silence that filled the room.

Things did not go as well for Jesus. At first, the crowd in the synagogue believed he was speaking about *them*, saying that he had come to liberate only the Israelites. As he continued talking, it became apparent that Jesus was talking *to* them, that this was a call to take action, not receive it. He would be moving along to save other people. Luke writes, "When they heard this, all in the synagogue were filled with wrath. And they rose up ... and led him to the brow of the hill on which their city was built, that they might throw him down headlong. But passing through the midst of them he went away."

This scripture, minus the cliff-throwing ordeal, has remained a favorite for ministers like Sam who demand social or political action. While I was searching through his archives file, I found a brochure whose photographs were captioned with Bible verses. Under the heading, "Your church reaches out...through pastoral ministry," is a picture of Sam preaching in the sanctuary, the image of a white man in the early '60s—short hair, thick black glasses, and a thin tie with a tidy knot. The Bible verse beside his photo is the same text Jesus read in Nazareth.

Sam's widow told me that of all the sermons her husband burned, she'd most like to have the ones from Calvary back. "I think he did his best preaching there." If he'd confined himself to the pulpit, perhaps things would have turned out differently. But throughout the early '60s, as white mobs were burning buses and bombing churches across the South, as the demand for a Voting Rights Act reached fever pitch, Sam was hitting the streets. He was frequently downtown marching, or in segregated restaurants near Calvary, where activist whites would hold "sip-ins." Rosemary Brown, Calvary's Associate Pastor at the time, giggled girlishly over the phone as she told me about sip-ins at the Pancake Pantry, which is still the most popular breakfast spot in Green Hills and my favorite restaurant. "We filled all their tables and then they couldn't get any good business. We'd drink enough coffee to kill a horse." Sam and Rosemary were even arrested once for blocking an interchange during a protest. Calvary started getting hate mail and bomb threats. The congregation became increasingly uneasy. After a Birmingham church bombing killed four black youths in 1963, Sam and other local clergy marched to City Hall in protest. Weeks later, Gov. Frank Clement, who attended Calvary, formed a Commission on Human Relations to work on civil rights issues. He asked Sam to chair the commission.

Sam accepted the post, and all the tension that had slowly accrued over the years at Calvary reached its tipping point. "Now, that's when the Calvary church became very, very upset," Helen told me. No one overtly cited racial issues. Instead, the battle was cloaked under concerns that Sam had accepted the post without consulting the church board. But the Governor's post was an unpaid position. "It did take up some of his time," one church member told me, "but an appointment to a similar position with the Red Cross or United Way would have caused no such trouble."

In the archives I found a letter from a group of people calling themselves the Committee on Social Concerns. The letter referred to Sam's recent acceptance of the chairman's position and recommended he be demoted to Assistant Pastor. "Calvary, indeed every church, requires leadership, personal leadership, concerned for the problems of all members of its family. It does not seem possible that it can have this leadership if its minister feels obliged from personal convictions to spend more and more of his time away from his congregation—and especially if he feels that he is no longer able to reach all members of his church with compassion and understanding."

Before 1964 came to an end, St. Paul Southern Methodist Church had its charter.

### I GAVE UP CHILDISH WAYS, 1992

Eventually, time will erase the trench Confederate soldiers dug 142 years ago for the battle on what are now the Calvary grounds. It's shallower than it was originally, covered in vines and brush with two trees growing from it. As the church has expanded, care has been taken not to build over it, but no one's going to re-dig it, either. When I was a teenager at Calvary, the redoubt was simply a part of our landscape. At that time, it was in the side yard of the rundown house that served as the youth Sunday school building. In the evenings, playing Frisbee, we had to be careful not to fall in. The slave wall out front is different. They are common in southwest Nashville—well-maintained, silent memorials to those who built them. But we don't really notice them either.

All of us must have tromped right past the redoubt one morning when we left Sunday school, climbed into the church van, and headed downtown to worship at an inner city Methodist church. I remember that van ride as similar to so many others we took in junior high—noisy. We were dressed in church clothes, glad to get a break from our usual Sunday routine, and gave little thought to where we were going. For us, the troubles between blacks and whites were as ancient and invisible as the history on Calvary's grounds. Then we stepped out of our van and into the heart of black Nashville. I don't remember much about what I saw at that moment. I can't remember which of my friends I walked beside, or what I was wearing. What I do remember was the absolute silence as we moved across the parking lot.

There were a dozen of us, all junior high kids, and no one spoke a word. We walked in a clump, inches from each other. At one point, I gazed over all the blonde and brown heads to the neighborhood beyond. It was a warm day, and I could see dark faces through many open doorways. One man stood behind his screen door in his undershirt, resting an elbow on the doorjamb, staring at our little knot of white humanity as we made our way to the church door. I quickly turned away and kept my eyes glued to the backs of our four adult leaders. We opened the side door and ducked inside.

Their sanctuary was much smaller than Calvary's, more of an A-frame than an arch, with exposed brown beams. The windows were smaller, too. Not as much light. But some things were familiar—the altar with a cross and communion bread covered in white linen. My memory fails me here. The scripture readings, the sermon, and the specific hymns we sang have all been lost to time. What remains is my feeling of being completely swept into the energy of the service, yet a little baffled that something as familiar as a Methodist worship could seem so different.

I was interested in all kinds of music when I was a teenager, and at Calvary I was one of the few young people who actually sang during the hymns. At Clark, we were all singing. The choir swayed and some of us swayed too, hardly aware of it, unable to stay still. We watched the choir, felt the weight of a hymnal steady across our palms, and sang. The hymnal. I'd sung from one every Sunday for most of my life, but I'd never heard a congregation like Clark's. After a couple of hymns, the service shifted to announcements, or the Old Testament reading, I can't remember exactly, but it was something that wasn't quite as engrossing as the singing. Brandon and I, still full of the energy we'd felt in the music, couldn't listen. We hunched over a hymnal trying to figure out if it was the same one we used at Calvary.

"It says United Methodist Hymnal on the front," I whispered, "It must be the same. They wouldn't segregate the hymnals."

"I've just never heard hymns sound like this," he said.

We tried to read the music and decided that it was probably the same hymnal because hymn #666 was "Shalom to You," just as it was in Calvary's, but we weren't completely certain. We just couldn't get over the difference, the question: "Are they singing the same music as us?"

## "SAM DODSON NOW KNOWS THE SCORE" (*THE CARTHAGE COURIER*, MAY 21, 1964)

The Calvary Board, which determines a minister's salary and appointment status, told the Methodist bishop in 1964 that they did not want Sam to continue leading Calvary. The bishop refused to move him, so the Board cut Sam's salary by $1,000. I only know this because Helen told me. The relevant Board meeting minutes are missing from the archives. There's an angry letter from the bishop about the Board's decision to fire Sam, but no record of any discussion of Sam's employment in the minutes.

Sam stayed on another year, continuing to preach out of his convictions. He also drafted a code of fair employment practices for the state government. In May 1965, he received an offer to serve at the St. Andrew's American Church in Athens, Greece. He moved there with his family that August, but before he left, Calvary held a reception in his honor and gave him a check for over $2,000 that had been collected from the congregation. A photo from the religion page in *The Tennessean* shows Sam accepting the money from the board chairman, surrounded by his family. Everyone grins so falsely it looks like a car ad.

The Dodsons stayed in Greece until 1968. When they returned to the States, Sam was appointed to a church in Kentucky, where they lived for 10 years. After Sam retired in 1978, they moved back to Nashville, which had always been home to them. Helen told me she wanted to join Calvary, "But Sam said, 'Now, you know we can't do that.'" So they became members at West End Methodist, a church with a similar demographic about four miles away.

This is where Sam's funeral was held in March 2002, a month after Calvary celebrated its 60th Anniversary. The Dodsons had planned to attend the celebration in the sanctuary. There, they would have been publicly recognized for their service to the church for the first time since that photo ran in the *Tennessean*. Instead, Sam was taken to the hospital that very Sunday morning. There was never a public, mutual gesture of reconciliation, but the current minister, Peter, did devote a column to Sam in the church newspaper, praising him for taking a stand during difficult times.

How should Calvary handle this chapter in its past? Helen attends Calvary every week now although she is in her 90s and nearly deaf.

She speaks frequently with Peter and plays bridge with members of her Sunday school class—people who have been her friends since Sam started on at Calvary over 50 years ago. Sometimes, she said, older members come up to her and tell her that Sam was just ahead of his day, that they understand now.

When I was in the balcony on New Year's Day, she sat below me in the congregation. After the service ended, she smelled the same wax and smoke, walked through the same doors, and shook the minister's hand. Almost certainly, someone wished her a good week. Helen's not angry about the past; no one I spoke with seems to be. It was so long ago, they say, and Calvary is a good church. It is. Calvary is a place where children roam the hallways in packs, where teenagers feel secure and loved. It is a place where adults make friends and keep them for their entire lives, until their children and children's children are friends as well. It is Calvary, and not school, where I learned to listen carefully and formulate my own opinions. Bible studies taught me to consider history, to examine issues from all perspectives. All the while, Sam's story was fading into the shadows, becoming faint like smoke wafting toward a vaulted ceiling. If I am the first to try to piece this story back together, what have we lost?

## FOR NOW WE SEE INTO A MIRROR DIMLY, BUT THEN FACE TO FACE, 1992

Before my youth group friends and I left the sanctuary of Clark Memorial United Methodist Church, we lined up and shook hands with the congregation, as is the custom with visitors. We were greeted warmly. Walking back to our van, I noticed something remarkable. We were exuberant. Chattering, we fanned out across the parking lot. I leapt into the air, holding my dress down with one hand and stretching for a tree leaf with the other. My shoes slipped off and I was barefoot when I landed, the warm asphalt beneath my arches. This is how we behaved at Calvary. We felt, for a few brief moments on that distant Sunday, like we were home.

It was March. In a few weeks the riots in L.A. would begin, revealing to all of America the true depth of our trenches, but I, through that ordeal, tried to remember the waxy new leaf I'd pulled off that tree. The laughter around me. The tight, close feeling of that sanctuary. And the music.

I know now that local civil rights leaders met at Clark in the 1960s and I'm grateful that the place where leaders once preached and prayed for freedom from prejudice also released us, for one spring morning, from ours.

# LEARNING GLORY

*Gloria* is Latin for *glory*, a small word with grand implications. We hear it most often at Christmas, but glory is more than a word in a seasonal chorus. It is "majesty or splendor," "praise and thanksgiving offered as an act of worship to a deity," or "a halo around somebody's head." Glory is "beauty that inspires wonder and joy." It can also be an interjection. This is a dated usage, but still, I hear it. Somewhere, at this moment, a papery voice says, "Well, glory be!" into a telephone, and the world rights itself. Glory.

The Gloria is a liturgy in the Christian church, its words based on the scriptural account of the angels' song the night Christ was born. It is sung in Latin or English. *Glory to God in the highest! And on earth peace to men of good will.* In Catholic Mass, the Gloria is sung nearly every Sunday of the year, usually after the Kyrie and before the Opening Prayer. It is meant to be joyous, because each Sunday, after all, is an anniversary celebration of the day Christ rose from the dead.

There are 10 Sundays when the Gloria is not recited. Six are during Lent, the season that begins in ashes and ends in lilies. The others are during Advent, the four weeks leading up to Christmas. It's easy to forget that this is meant to be a solemn time commemorating the millennia people waited for a Messiah, but that's the whole point—to remember the wait, and be aware that we are still waiting for Him to come again.

Because it is part of the Mass and very nearly as old as the Church itself, many major composers have arranged a Gloria. Vivaldi composed one, as did Handel and Poulenc. Mozart and Bach would have penned one Gloria for nearly every Mass they composed. The full Gloria is 17 sentences long. When sung or chanted, it requires anywhere from two to thirty minutes, depending on the arrangement. John Rutter, an Englishman, composed one Gloria, first performed in 1974. It is 17 minutes and 28 seconds long and was printed in a red songbook with the title embossed in gold on the front cover. This is what the choir's librarian handed me on the last Wednesday in September in 1993. I was 15 at the time, a soprano, and one of two teenagers in the Sanctuary Choir at my church.

Dr. Farnsley, our director, began to talk about the music after we'd all received our songbooks. We'd be singing Rutter's Gloria for our annual Christmas festival on the third Sunday of Advent, he said. I flipped through the pages, searching for familiar hymns. Being Methodist and fairly ignorant of liturgies and masses, the songbook's title reminded me of angel carols I'd sung. "Angels We Have Heard on High" had been my sixth-grade saxophone solo. Amy Grant sings it on her first Christmas album, the one my family always listened to whenever we drove out to Opryland for the Country Christmas light display. "Hark! The Herald Angels Sing!" is both stately and joyful, a song that invites loud singing in the pews. I'd loved that scene where the Peanuts gang sings it in "A Charlie Brown Christmas." Frank Sinatra and Perry Como have each sung it. Their dulcet tones emanated from the record player in my house and followed me among the rows of jaunty, sweatered mannequins in the Green Hills mall.

So, Dr. Farnsley talked and I searched for my own answers. The first pages of Rutter's Gloria were in Latin. Not unusual. The next pages were in Latin, too. I flipped faster, trying to find the point where the Latin stopped and the familiar hymns began. Dr. Farnsley rambled on. I reached the back cover, frowned, and turned the pages more slowly. Dr. Farnsley raised his arms and pressed the thumb and index finger of each hand together. "Let's just try the first page," he said.

---

At 15, I thrived on motion. I played soccer, was in speech and band, took advanced classes, and drank instant coffee. My parents initially didn't want me to sing in the choir because I was doing so much already. But I insisted. I liked singing. I'd spent my Sundays listening to the Sanctuary Choir, the call and response across the chancel, the lilt and rumble of their voices. Dr. Farnsley had only invited two teenagers to join. My parents relented. I added Wednesday night rehearsals to my list of activities. Every week, I rode the city bus from school to the Green Hills library, studied for a few hours, and then walked up the hill to church.

Every Sunday, I sang. I liked the swish of the robes as we walked to the sanctuary with our music tucked under one arm. The congregation was vast, our sanctuary long and white, but I felt comfortable and anonymous standing in front of the church with just my pumps sticking out beneath the hem of my grey robe. Meanwhile, my voice was a single instrument seeking to blend. All my motion became disciplined and productive as I worked my diaphragm like a bellows, pulled out the stops. At the end of our weekly offertory, Dr. Farnsley would smile and nod to us. We sang the Doxology, closed our folders, and took our seats in one movement.

---

When singing in Latin, it's important to remember that the syllables and accents come differently than they would in English.

"It's *'Glow—rriah een,'*" Dr. Farnsley said, "Not *'Glor-riuh in.'*" He raised his arms again.

During the early rehearsals, we simply tried to understand the sound and motion of the piece. We were supposed to be angels, but our early attempts at singing Rutter's Gloria gave the piece the plod and thump of a donkey ride. Often, Dr. Farnsley made us put down our songbooks and clap the rhythm. *Et een ter-raa pax*, he'd say and I'd rock back on two legs of my chair, stifling a yawn. The room was always too warm. The dull green carpet smelled musty. Our robes, which were the color of dry pavement, hung across one wall. Cubbies covered the other wall. In between, along the back, were metal filing cabinets filled with enough music to sustain us through decades of Sundays. Sometimes, I would get a sheet of music so old it was yellow and soft as cotton. Some previous soprano had written notes to herself, like "watch" or "diminuendo," in delicate script and there seemed something lonely and tenacious about the black notes and fading pencil lead.

I never considered quitting during those first, tedious Gloria rehearsals. I loved singing, the ability it gave me to be centered and dynamic at the same time. And I had three close friends in the choir. Brandon, who was also 15, had been my friend since I was four. Brandon was tall. He sang tenor and wore round wire-rimmed glasses. During our Christmases together in the Children's Choir, he and I had donned bathrobes and sung from the back row, because we were the loudest. During the Gloria Christmas, we shot hoops in the gym before practice and complained about Algebra 2 and unrequited crushes. Eddie and Lynn were our former junior high youth counselors. Eddie sang bass and Lynn alto. They were from West Virginia and had a slight tinge of mountain in their voices. When Eddie and Lynn drove me home after practice, I had an audience for stories about soccer games, weekend adventures, and overbearing teachers. I figured I could tolerate some Latin between basketball and the ride home.

Dr. Farnsley ordered cassettes of *Gloria: The Sacred Music of John Rutter* for each of us. We were to listen, he said, and get a feel for the time signatures and accents, the crescendos, decrescendos, and *poco a pocos*. I spun the cassette case between my fingertips while I spoke with Eddie in the car that night. The Christmas before, we'd sung a dozen familiar hymns for the festival. We and I had made up verses to "The Friendly Beasts" with words like, *I, said the hippo, all fat and wide*, and sniggered into our sheet music during practice.

This Christmas was not going the same way. This Latin piece just seemed like it would be, "Dull and flat," I said. The nighttime scenery shifted from gas stations to subdivisions to the streetlights in my neighborhood. We spoke to the windshield or each other's profile. Eddie and Lynn commiserated with me more often than they rejoindered. However, that night, Eddie said he believed that Rutter's Gloria would be "pretty fun to do." I nodded, silently dismissing his comment as the type of thing adults feel obligated to say. We turned right on Robert E. Lee Drive. When I got home, I set the cassette tape on the far corner of my desk, flipped open my Algebra book, and tried to remember what Brandon had said about imaginary numbers.

---

Telesphorus, who was martyred in 137, was the first Pope to order the inclusion of the Gloria in the liturgy. It would have been recited in Greek at that time and borne little resemblance to what is sung today. However, the Gloria has always been based on the angels' song from the second chapter of Luke. When did I first hear that story? Shepherds were in a field. An angel appeared and told them to go to Bethlehem. Then, more angels appeared—a *host*, the Bible says—and they praised God. When the angels were done, the shepherds decided to do what they'd said. This all takes no more than an inch of the tiny print in my Bible.

But someone decided to expand on the angels' song in the second century. Pope Telesphorus put it into the Mass. Now, the story is ubiquitous. *Do you hear what I hear? Hark! The herald angels sing!* Through our collective childhoods, my sister and I played every conceivable minor part, plus Mary, in the church Christmas musicals. Always a different character and a slightly jazzed up plot—the children tell the fourth wise man about Jesus, the children travel back in time—but always the same dark blue bathrobe with white trim—our father's. The Gloria's text as it is now, as most of us know it, isn't quite as old as the one Telesphorus commissioned. Ours only dates from the ninth century.

---

The Rutter tape remained on my desk, buried, uncovered, and reburied by the shifting tides of my homework, for a couple weeks. When I realized I couldn't keep up with the other sopranos anymore, I gave in, popped the cassette into my Walkman one day in October, and carried it to school. I put on my headphones during study hall. The first movement sounded staccato and harsh, just as it had in practice. Dr. Farnsley had called it dissonance: *Glow! Ri-ah! In ex-cel-sis De! O!* I wanted "Angels We Have Heard on High," and the pleasant carols where *Gloria* lifts and builds across 18 syllables. But something in that first movement seemed so directed and driven that I kept listening.

The second movement was slower, beginning with the organ sounding like flutes far away in a dark room. The tenors and basses sang *Dómine Deus Rex cæléstis,* drawing each syllable out, climbing. Then the altos sang *Deus Pater omnípotens.* The sopranos climbed even higher with *Dómine Fili unigénite, Jesu Christe, Jesu Christe.* I didn't know exactly what the words meant, only that they seemed so beautiful, yet pleading, and they gave me chills. Finally, the third movement began. Trumpets, a xylophone, the deep pounding of timpani, and the words: *Quóniam tu solus Sanctus. Tu solus Dóminus, Tu solus Altíssimus, Jesu Christe,* which the sopranos and altos sang in harmony. The basses and tenors responded. It was nearly all eighth and sixteenth notes, rapid and jubilant. I began to smile. When it ended, I hit rewind. I did this again and again. My unrequited crush asked me what I was listening to. He was wearing a Dead Kennedys t-shirt.

"Oh, just something I have to learn for choir," I said.

He turned around. I hit rewind and tried to keep my face grim.

I was a Walkman kid, incapable of taking more than a few steps without my own soundtrack. That fall, I listened to Rutter's Gloria as

I walked the hallways between classes. The halls were anonymous but churning, like me. I felt like the music sounded—calm but driven, joyous but desperate. I listened to Rutter's Gloria in the van on the speech club trip to Cincinnati. I lay on my narrow bunk at the youth group fall retreat and allowed the second movement to lull me to sleep; the third played while I dressed for breakfast. I put it in the tape deck of my parents' car even if we were only driving to the corner store.

By November in Nashville, the sun sets at 4:30 and it rains regularly. That fall, I listened to Rutter's Gloria every week while rain lashed the windows of the city bus and made streaks in the grime. I noticed that the water droplets distorted the streetlights. It seemed as though each one had a dull golden halo around it.

---

The Gloria we recognize at Masses today was sung in plainchant before any composer set it. Chants have no instrumentation, key signatures, or time signatures. They are unison; there are no sopranos, altos, tenors, or basses. When written, they resembled shape notes. Medieval monks chanted their prayers this way every day. They chanted them in small monasteries and in the great Cathedrals that took lifetimes to build. Parishioners could not understand the Latin, but the sound enveloped them.

Rutter's Gloria is primarily in 3/4 time. The score calls for four trumpets, two tenor trombones, one bass trombone, a tuba, percussion, and an organ. On the Wednesday before the festival, the Wednesday before Christmas break, all those instrumentalists were in the chancel at Calvary. The choir sat in pews, the men and women facing each other on either side of the altar. The organ pipes arched above us, and the instrumentalists covered the red-carpeted space between the groups of pews.

After so many bathrobe musicals, I was surprised the church had splurged for the session musicians. Paid by the hour, there was no chit-chat before practice, only valve cleaning and stern faces. Eddie and Brandon sat rigidly in pews across the chancel. Lynn was in front of me. There would be no parody verses—only Rutter's Gloria stirring within me, blending with the other voices. Only that and the dim, empty sanctuary, the pews, the ceiling's shallow arch.

Outside was rain and traffic. Inside was the space I knew as well as breathing, the pews in which we'd sat, slumped, and sang, the altar where we knelt and drank grape juice, all of it filled with sound and transformed. The beginning was triumphant and colliding. The middle so pleading and sad that the entire world seemed a thing the sanctuary could not protect us from. The ending was joyous. We worked hardest on the last two pages. It's mainly *Amen*, over and over, but the different sections call out to each other and the time signature switches from 3/4 to 5/8 to 3/8, so it sounds like a train accelerating, and everything is motion. The soprano part was like climbing a ladder or treading water. Dr. Farnsley waved his arms, I took deep breaths and watched him, having memorized the music long before.

---

The following Wednesday, Brandon and I sat next to Eddie and Lynn's son, Chris, at the annual Christmas Family Dinner in the church gym. He was in kindergarten, a fountain of energy even when it wasn't three days before Christmas. As we ate, he told knock-knock jokes and sang every novelty Christmas tune he knew. I was wearing my school's rugby jersey, conspicuously blue and white amid the red and green. It was a co-ed rugby club, so our games were often no more than an elaborate flirting ritual—that afternoon, we'd tumbled all over each other singing "The Holly and the Ivy," and imitating Frank Sinatra. The lyrics were accentuated with hits, fumbles, and falls. My dad, sister, and I still had presents to buy, and my family was going to drive around looking at Christmas lights that evening. There were 10 days of break left, but I knew what Lynn meant when she said, "I can't believe it's over."

---

I wonder what language the angels sang in when they told the shepherds to go to Bethlehem. Probably not Latin. The Romans were occupiers. Perhaps Hebrew, the ancient and holy language of the Jews. As a sacred tongue, surely God's messengers would have employed it. But maybe the shepherds didn't spend enough time in synagogues to know Hebrew. Maybe the angels sang in Aramaic, the language Jesus spoke. Or perhaps it was a song without words and the shepherds, dazzled and shivering, understood what they were meant to do.

This is what *we* understood on the night we sang Rutter's Gloria for the 1993 Festival of Lights: When we processed in to "O Come, All Ye Faithful," we could see the choir loft surrounded in poinsettias. Above them, candles capped in gold. On the walls, wreaths dressed with red ribbon. When the orchestra entered and the brass began to play, the loft shimmered in gold and music.

I snuck a sip of ice water. The first movement was loud. I could see heads bowed in the congregation, studying the English translation in the bulletin. *Grátias ágimus tibi*, the women sang—*We give you thanks*. The men rumbled back, *Propter magnam glóriam tuam*—*For your great glory*. Then we spilled over each other for another round of *Gloria in excelsis deo*, the trumpets had an accented triplet plus a quarter note and, suddenly, there was silence. The orchestra turned their pages. The organ's flutey sound began the second movement.

*Domine Deus*, we sang over and over again—*Lord God* and the music built under us, the trumpets nearly overpowered us, *Domine Deus, Domine Deus* we crescendoed, pleading. *Rex cæléstis*—*Heavenly Father* was fortissisimo, a desperate, high A-flat for sopranos. Then we were silent. The trumpets crescendoed, but then they stopped, too, and it was like that second when you jump and one toe still touches Earth. *Lord God, Heavenly Father* hung in the silence like a prayer. Outside, the traffic was streaming by, the world was spinning on its axis, pencil marks were erased from a book, someone was sobbing against a bus window, only two Salvation Army angels remained on the tree at the mall—all of this in that ringing silent moment. Then the altos continued, slowly, with no instruments above them—*Qui tollis peccáta mundi, You who take away the sins of the world*. One soprano sang *Miserere nobis*, then we all joined her *Have mercy upon us*. There was no orchestra, only our voices. The organ flutes came in for a few slow bars before all music stopped.

But the angels' song, according to the scripture, was full of joy and splendor. It *was* glory. The shepherds shivered from cold and wonder on a hillside near Bethlehem, someone told the story, someone put it to music. We sang the third movement in a church sanctuary in 1993, beginning with the trumpets' fortissimo. *Quóniam tu solus Sanctus, Tu solus Dominus, Tu solus Altissimus*—*For you alone are the holy one, you alone are the Lord, you alone are the most high*. The words mingled with the trumpets and every section had a soli. The final movement was four minutes long, but the *Amens* began after about two. They were sung in counter-rhythm to each other until it all sounded like cascading light.

And then it was only us, the sopranos on a high C—*A-men!* Inside, everything I had was reaching, projecting. At last, the cut-off and a breath. The trumpets and timpani gave four short blasts. The Gloria had ended. Outside Bethlehem, the sky closed like a river flowing over a log and then even that was gone, and the shepherds stood alone in the dark.

# DEFORD'S BLUES

**ELVIRA**

The first song I clearly remember loving was in the Top 40 rotation the summer I turned three.

My parents had a radio alarm clock with white numbers printed on little sheets of black tin. Every morning, when the numbers clicked to 6:15, the radio came on. I listened, in bed between my parents, as the man on the radio began to talk. When Mom and Dad got up, leaving wide divots of warmth on either side of me, I stayed under the covers. The blankets muffled the grown-up voice on the radio and the garbled, tooth-brushing voices of my parents. Finally, a tinny, Western-style piano buzzed through the clock's speakers—the intro to my song. I kicked off the blankets and leapt to the floor just in time for: *El-VI-ruh, El-VI-ruh. My heart's on fy-ah for El-VI-ruh.* While Mom and Dad hurried between their closets and the bathroom, I curled my toes into the green carpet in front of the big window and bounced. When those Oak Ridge Boys sang: *Hi-ho, Silver, ay-wayy*, I yelled along.

Bouncing along one morning, I decided that "Elvira" must be the best song in the whole world. I already understood a lot about music when I was three years old. It was written by someone, performed by someone else, and told a story. I knew this because my mother sat downstairs in her office every day writing stories about music for magazines and my father played records and explained the stories in the music. I even had a record collection all my own: *Bedtime for Big Bird*, *Tom T. Hall's Country Songs for Children*, *Free to Be You and Me*, and *Christmas in Ireland with the Little Dublin Singers*. We lived in a place called Music City. Tom T. Hall lived there, too, and we visited his farm every Christmas for hayrides and cider.

On Sundays, while my parents made dinner after church, Dad played classical music and told me to listen for the stories. I loved to say, "Vivaldi," and to listen to his songs, which sounded like meadows and falling leaves. Grieg's "In the Hall of the Mountain King" sent me running up the stairs and under the covers. My mother wrote about country music and listened to it, too. She liked to play Willie Nelson, Emmylou Harris (who was as pretty as her voice), Loretta Lynn, and Dolly Parton, or groups she'd loved in college—The Association and The Doors. And when Gladys Knight sang about riding a train at midnight, my parents stopped everything and danced in their aprons.

---

My family's record collection is inseparable from my earliest memories, my first conceptions of a world beyond myself. The essayist Annie Dillard would call this the time I slid into my skin. The skin I filled as I became myself was fair and topped with nearly translucent blonde curls.

During the workday, I sat in the big easy chair in Mom's office and played while she typed. I banged at my toy typewriter and looked through the viewfinder of my Big Bird camera. The office where Mom wrote was nearly all windows, so I often retreated to the cool living room. There I watched "Sesame Street" or covertly played with the stereo cabinet—fanning its lovely smell of vinyl, cardboard, and needle cleanser across the room. In the summer, Mom took me to the pool. The Wildwood Swim and Tennis Club had a radio speaker right next to the Sun Drop clock. Whenever "Elvira" came on, everything stopped and all the kids danced in the water. I loved the sound of the words—*El-VI-ruh*! Even during that distant summer, there were echoes of what I would become.

About six miles from Wildwood, as I was slipping into my life, a man I did not know was beginning to slide out of his. As a boy, DeFord Bailey had lived on a farm like Tom T. Hall's, but by the time he was 81 and I was three, Mr. Bailey lived in an apartment in the I.W. Gernert public housing complex, surrounded with memorabilia from his life as a musician.

That DeFord Bailey lived in a subsidized apartment at the end of his life while the Oak Ridge Boys were watching their own star ascend is nearly tragic. Their "Elvira" was a crossover hit, a country music song that also appealed to mainstream pop music audiences. Bailey had appealed to radio listeners from all walks of life before the genre "country music" even existed. Along with his Grand Ole Opry co-stars, Bailey had set country music, and Nashville, on its path.

### MUSIC IN EVERYTHING

If it were not for David Morton, a young employee of the Nashville Housing and Development Authority, I can't help but wonder if we would have lost DeFord Bailey's story entirely. Bailey became a shoeshiner after he was dismissed from the Opry in 1941 and rarely performed or even discussed his career again. After he allowed Morton to do a short write-up for a public housing newsletter, a friendship developed between the two men. When Charles Wolfe wanted to write about Bailey for his book *The Grand Ole Opry: The Early Years*, Bailey was more willing than he might have been otherwise.

He joyously told both Morton and Wolfe about the music he had learned from his family in the early 1900s. Wolfe, a pre-eminent country music historian, wrote that he devoted much of his research after that day to what Bailey called "black hillbilly music." Through his work, Wolfe revealed what we should have remembered all along—Southern whites and blacks are culturally connected through slavery. They borrowed instruments and music from each other—the banjo, for example, came from Africa. Country music as we know it today is constructed equally from white and black.

Like me, young DeFord grew up in a family that loved music and stories. But unlike my own family, his actually played the music. After the Civil War, Bailey's grandparents, both ex-slaves, had settled in the craggy farmland around the Smith-Wilson county line, about 40 miles east of Nashville. The Baileys and their children worked with their hands all day as laborers and sharecroppers, and in the evenings, they pressed their callused fingertips onto frets. Their knuckles danced across piano keys. The Baileys were fiddlers, banjo players, pianists, mandolin players, buglers, singers, guitar players, and harmonica virtuosos.

When they carried their instruments to county fairs and barn dances, everyone cleared the stage to hear black hillbilly music. The Baileys entertained the farmers, black and white, with renditions of "Comin' Round the Mountain," and "John Henry." For Deford, string-band music was the real black music, straight out of Africa. Morton writes that Bailey often referred to blues and jazz as a "craze."

Born into the Bailey clan on a snowy night in the last month of the 19th century, Deford told his biographers that, as a baby, whenever he cried someone handed him a mandolin or a harmonica. His mother died while he was an infant and his father could not both earn a living and care for him. So DeFord's aunt, Barbara Lou Odum, took him in. She played guitar and sang. Her husband, Clark, played banjo, fiddle, and guitar. Grandfather Lewis, a champion fiddler, lived with them on their tenant farm.

DeFord was already able to play his harp when he caught polio at the age of three. He eventually learned to walk again, but not before he'd spent a year confined to his bed. As DeFord grew into his world, this is what he saw: his bed, the gleaming harmonica in his hands, and a window thrown open to all the sounds of a farmyard. He imitated those sounds with his harp—chickens, geese, mules, men hunting fox and the lonely whistle from the train known as the Nashville, Chattanooga, and St. Louis. "You know," he often said to Morton, "There's music in everything."

By the time he was well enough to walk again, Bailey carried his harp with him everywhere. He learned other instruments, too—the banjo and the fiddle. He wandered the cedar forests and creek banks around the farm and, as his ancestors had done since before slavery, made banjos from animal skins, fifes from cane, and pipes from reeds. Bailey shared with his biographers stories of his extended family gathering at the farmhouse in the evenings and playing their instruments by the fireplace. Grandfather Lewis' fiddle rattled with the snake's rattler he'd put inside. Lewis took the lead on "Sweet Marie," "The Preacher and the Bear," "Old Joe Clark," and "Alberta, Don't Grieve About a Dime."

Bailey learned to turn those fiddle tunes into harp tunes. Always sent to bed too early, he'd lie there in the dark with his cousins, all of them awake until the music ended. Heir to a rich musical tradition flowing back through slavery to Africa, he told Morton, "All them things was happiness back then."

Because of the polio, Bailey never grew over five feet tall. His family worried about him—how would he survive if he could not do hard labor? Bailey decided that, whatever he chose to do, it would involve music. In 1918, after working as a houseboy in rural Thompson's Station, Bailey decided to join his foster parents and siblings, who had recently moved to Nashville. The young man got on the train one autumn morning and got off in a second-rate southern city that was trying to gain some cultural credibility by building a full-scale replica of the Parthenon in its largest park and calling itself "The Athens of the South." The 18-year-old Bailey was not exactly a part of Nashville's hoped-for identity, not so much because he was black, but because he was rural. Nashville's established citizenry wanted the city to be a center for classical learning, not a gathering place for every dreamy-eyed hayseed in Tennessee.

When Bailey stepped into the Nashville streets that day, Roy Acuff was still a gangly mountain kid obsessed with dreams of playing professional baseball. Jimmie Rodgers was down South, working for the railroad alongside the steel drivers who would inspire him to write his classic, "Muleskinner Blues." Young Bill Monroe and his mandolin were up in the hills of Kentucky where another connoisseur of black hillbilly music, Arnold Schulz, was teaching him how to thumb pick and make "runs"—waterfalls of music across the eight strings. But Bailey was already in the town that would, with his help, become Music City.

Before long, music was his living. Bailey told his biographers that his employers, the prominent, old-money Bradford family, put him to work polishing silver and caring for the family Packard. One afternoon, Mrs. Bradford heard him playing his harp under a tree, and soon entertaining the family and their guests became his only job. Bailey, wearing fine suits and shiny shoes, stood in a corner of the dining room and played antebellum songs like "S'wanee River."

"From then on," Bailey said, "my work was playing the harp."

## CROSSOVER HITS

I got my own record player, a bombproof turntable in a heavy plastic carrying case, when I was about four. It was white with red and blue stripes. The needle itself was encased in heavy white plastic. My sister Cathleen's birth later that year ended my status as a younger, shorter, but otherwise equal member in a family of three. More and more children's music appeared in the house; my parents bought me read-along books with a little record tucked into the back cover. Those and "Disney's Happiest Tunes" spun incessantly on my turntable. My sister eventually received a cheap cassette player that she covered in crayon scribble. Though I wasn't a fan of the Raffi emanating from her room, I did enjoy her Wee Sing collection. I realize now that it had a number of folk songs Bailey would have played with his family; "It

Ain't Gonna Rain No More," in fact, was his first radio hit in Nashville.

After Cathleen was born in the spring of 1983, Mom didn't freelance as much. With all the excitement, I didn't notice right away that the typewriter was quiet for days at a time. Warner Brothers still sent us complimentary records at least twice a month. We didn't like them as much as the ones Mom had reviewed in the '70s and early '80s. Maybe country took a downswing after those days when you could hear old standards like Roy Acuff and newcomers like Barbara Mandrell all in the same night on the Opry. Maybe the music just lost its immediacy for us since Mom was no longer sharing stories at the supper table about interviewing Chet Atkins or visiting Loretta Lynn's ranch. In 1988, when Hank Williams, Jr.'s "If the South Had Only Won, We'd Have it Made" climbed the charts, my mother referred to country as "total crap" and the new stuff was rarely, if ever, played in our house again.

Music, however, was still a part of our lives and a part of the city where we lived. One of my mother's closest friends began dating the son of legendary songwriters Felice and Boudleaux Bryant. Mom searched out their songs—lots of Everly Brothers hits and the famous "Rocky Top." I was incredulous when she told me that Dane's parents had written Tennessee's state song. Somehow, I'd assumed it had originated from the hills themselves.

After I was finally granted access to my parents' record cabinet, I passed my turntable and children's records over to my sister. She listened to them until she developed a taste for musicals like "The Harvey Girls" and "Kiss Me, Kate." Mom and Dad bought her lots of Judy Garland at the used record shop, while the three of us almost exclusively chose Western or Irish music with an occasional Dire Straits album mixed in. We listened to The Chieftains' *Ballad of the Irish Horse*, The Clancy Brothers' *Bold Fenian Men*, The Riders in the Sky's *Saddle Pals*. I loved The Riders in the Sky, partly because we knew them and partly because of the yodeling. The Clancy Brothers' Irish folk tunes were nearly always about war, gambling, drinking, or some combination of the three. I didn't understand the meaning of the words, but they seemed so beautiful. *Moonshine, dear moonshine, oh how I love thee!* I'd sing, or, *A small bird sat on an ivy bunch and the song he sang was a jug of punch.*

Dad still listened to classical music, but he rediscovered his love for Big Band jazz one day after digging his clarinet, saxophone, and flute out of a back room. When he taught me about classical music he was level and patient, but he worked himself into a frenzy over Benny Goodman, Count Basie, Lester Young, and Glen Miller. "Listen, listen to that!" He'd jump up from the couch and point into the air as though the music was clamoring visibly over our heads. "Do you know how hard it is to do that?" I loved it all—the country western, the Irish, the Big Band, even the musicals. By the time I was nine, I wouldn't have known Madonna or Debbie Gibson if they'd knocked on the front door and asked Dad to tell them about the straight triplets in "Tuxedo Junction."

And I understood these genres as separate. I carried my own version of American music's foundational myth somewhere deep within myself. I pictured Irish music crossing the ocean and settling in East Tennessee, then getting buffed and contorted into bluegrass and country, which crossed the frontier with the cowboys. Jazz had its separate line. It came up from New Orleans, brassy and wild, and stopped off in Memphis and Chicago to get a little polish or catch the blues. Distinct heritages for distinct music. White and black right there, taking separate spins on our turntable.

### THE PAN-AMERICAN BLUES, 1920S

In Nashville, the music business is referred to as The Industry. Like other industries around the country—steel, timber, coal—Nashville's has its legendary characters, its John Henrys and Paul Bunyans. There is, for example, the story of the first broadcast of the show that would become the Grand Ole Opry: On the night of November 28, 1925, Uncle Jimmy Thompson, a white-haired, obstinate mountain man, parked his homemade camper outside the fledgling WSM studio, took a tour of the station, and told the station's program director, George D. "Judge" Hay, that he wanted to play his fiddle into the microphone. The old man claimed a repertoire of hundreds of fiddle tunes, songs like "Red Wing," "Nubbin' Ridge," "Flying Clouds" and "Old Dan Tucker." He sat in front of the WSM microphone and played nonstop for an hour. By the time he put down his fiddle that night, WSM claimed to have received a telegram from listeners in all 48 states and Puerto Rico.

That is the version we like to believe in Nashville, infused as it is with romance and a mysterious mountain-man edge. I always picture a rainy night, even though the signal could only have carried as far as it did on a clear evening, and a man walking into the studio clutching a fiddle and bow in one knobby hand. Parts of the Uncle Jimmy myth are true. He was a hard-drinking fiddler who traveled the country in a homemade camper with his wife. He did play on the air one Saturday night. The occasion is now heralded as the birth of the Grand Ole Opry. WSM did receive telegrams from across the country as listeners requested fiddle tunes. But the truer story of the founding of the Grand Ole Opry begins this way: Judge Hay, WSM's new program director, was looking for a good way to sell life insurance.

WSM, after all, stands for "We Shield Millions," the slogan of the National Life and Accident Insurance Company. National Life had established the station and built a massive tower south of town to send a 5,000-watt signal across the U.S. On clear, cool nights, it could be heard in every state. In the mid-1920s, with incomes up and more people migrating to urban areas, the market was ripe, and National Life executives decided to reach their potential policyholders through radio.

But first, people needed a reason to tune in. Hay brought in a variety of musicians throughout the work week—classical, opera, and tight vocal choruses. He decided to anchor his Saturday night with a barn dance. Radio stations across the nation had barn dance shows, all of them designed to attract the scores of listeners who had moved from the country to the city during the 1920s. These new city dwellers desired "old-time music" to remind them of their younger days, when they'd attended county fairs and barn dances. Farmers, black and white, wanted to hear the music, too, because it reminded them of bucolic times when their children weren't leaving for the city by the trainload.

Hay knew the barn dance format would work, but he needed performers. Uncle Jimmy did not come staggering out of the hills. His niece, Eva, was WSM's classical pianist.

---

Here is another Music City legend. This one is mostly true: One Saturday night in November 1927, NBC was broadcasting its syndicated *Musical Appreciation Hour* on WSM. Near the end of the show, the host announced that he was about to make an exception to his belief that there was no room for realism in the classics; he then proceeded to broadcast an orchestral piece that mimicked an approaching locomotive.

Meanwhile, in Nashville, Judge Hay was standing by with the musicians for *The WSM Barn Dance*. As the symphonic locomotive chugged and whined through the final moments of the broadcast, Hay, with his knack for seizing the moment, summoned his best harmonica player to his side. The orchestral train faded out, the hour changed, and it was time for listeners across the South to hear the Barn Dance. Hay announced, "For the next three hours, we will present nothing but realism. It will be down to earth for the earthy."

He stepped away from the mic and the harmonica player swung into a rendition of his composition, "The Pan-American Blues," which evoked every train sound the orchestra had, and did so using only one man and one instrument. At the end of the song, Hay stepped back to the microphone. "For the past hour we have been listening to music taken largely from Grand Opera," he said, "But from now on we will present 'The Grand Ole Opry.'" Thus it was that DeFord Bailey, 27 years old by then and standing on a Coca-Cola crate to reach the microphone, helped name what is now the longest continuously-running radio show in America and the most venerable institution in white Southern music.

According to historical accounts, the Opry enjoyed remarkable success due to its signal strength and Hay's dogged image-building. By the end of the 1920s, every band in the show had a down-home name culled from a list Hay kept in his desk. Dr. Humphrey Bate and his Augmented String Orchestra became Dr. Bate and the Possum Hunters. The Dixie Clodhoppers and the Fruit Jar Drinkers were also frequent performers on the show.

For nearly a decade, Bailey was the Opry's most popular musician. Hay referred to him on-air as "The Harmonica Wizard," and once told Bailey, "You're nothing but a gold mine walking around on this earth." Here was a man, a black man, who played roots music right off the farm. His songs had titles like "Fox Chase" and "Old Hen Cackle." Bailey, who blacks somehow knew was black—while whites usually assumed he was white—became a huge draw for the Opry. He helped National Life sell a lot of insurance. In 1928, Bailey played in 49 of the 52 weekly broadcasts. Dr. Bate, dubbed "The Dean of the Opry," came in second behind Bailey with 25 weekly appearances. Uncle Dave Macon, "The Dixie Dew Drop," considered today to be the Opry's first real star, was a close third.

In the fall of 1928, executives from Victor records came through town to record the local talent. DeFord Bailey, the Binkley Brothers' Clodhoppers, and Paul Warmack and His Gully Jumpers became the first artists to cut commercial recordings in Nashville.

### HONOR THY MUSIC, 2006

Last June I did some research in the library at the Country Music Hall of Fame downtown. From my desk, I could see out across a city that looked considerably cleaner and brighter than the one I remember from my childhood. Across the street, some teenagers in turquoise we-are-tourists t-shirts played Frisbee on the lawn of a shiny new Hilton. No doubt they had already gone through the museum and been bored. I would have been bored, too, when I was teenager. The history of my town and its music didn't interest me, nor did the tourists who regularly waddled past my high school on the way to gift shops and honky tonks on Lower Broad. I still appreciated my parents' Irish folk and Big Band, but I lived in the moment when I was in high school, and that moment was comprised nearly entirely of R.E.M., with some U2, Paul Simon, Indigo Girls, Pearl Jam, They Might Be Giants, and Beatles thrown in for good measure.

At the magnet schools I attended from seventh grade on, music was the only thing that we felt comfortable dividing along racial lines. We were overt about it, both whites and blacks. We teased each other. An African-American friend of mine deejayed at most of the school dances. Joey was so much the embodiment of cool that I wondered why he even talked to me, but I didn't like the R&B, like Boyz II Men, that he played at school dances. When he saw my friend and me approaching the table where he'd set up his equipment, he'd say, "Oh, be patient, I'll play your white music in a few minutes." Paula and I would simply smile and nod, then disappear back into the dark, waiting for "Stand" or "Blister in the Sun." Sometimes we approached Joey with specific requests.

"'Yellow Submarine?'" he said once. "I am *not* playing 'Yellow Submarine.' Oh lord, you white kids with The Beatles. You can request another song of theirs, but I am *not* playing any 'Yellow Submarine.'"

In the hallways, during lunch at my high school, my white friends and I would frequently circle around whoever was going through the singer/songwriter phase which so often afflicts Nashville's white teenagers. While the aspiring musician strummed a new Fender acoustic, we sang "Free Fallin'" or "Mother Nature's Son." Further down the hall, a group of black kids would likely also have gathered, but they mostly danced. They called it stepping. The guys drummed and flipped their small fraternity canes in rhythm while the girls clapped or danced. My friends and I watched, amazed and perplexed, from our little gathering place. Sometimes, one group or the other would send out a kind of sentry and we'd be integrated for about five minutes. But the different musical styles were simply too far out of our collective comfort zones. Over 50 years after Bailey had been fired from the Opry, 90 years since he'd laid in his bed listening to his family's string band jam sessions, Nashville's music was as segregated as it had ever been.

I was finally allowed to drive myself to high school during my senior year. I'd pick up my friend Austin and we'd travel from our suburban life into the city. We listened exclusively to two radio stations—Lightning 100, which played an eclectic blend of music from the '60s to the present, and Thunder 94, which stuck mainly to groups like the Pixies and the Ramones. We didn't speak much. We only stopped for coffee, listened to the music, and hoped the lights would go our way so that we could park in the cheapest lot. I knew we were at the halfway point when we passed a historical marker by the housing projects on Edgehill, but I never read the marker. If I had taken the time, I would have seen these words: *Harmonica Wizard DeFord Bailey, the first star of the Grand Ole Opry, operated a shoeshine stand at this site from 1965 until his death in 1982.*

That day in June when I sat in the library at the Hall of Fame, I wondered if the tourists below me were surprised at the big Ray Charles exhibit. The people who bought those Hall of Fame t-shirts with "Honor Thy Music," did they believe their mother church was white?

### DEFORD ON THE ROAD

In the 1930s, the Opry was gaining national prominence. Bailey, who had a wife and three children to feed, began touring with other Opry stars. This was the first time many white fans realized their favorite harmonica player was black. But the crowds still turned out across the South to hear the Harmonica Wizard playing in high school gymnasiums and night clubs. I wonder, sometimes, if his traveling show ever passed through Fayette, Alabama, my grandmother's hometown. She would have been in her early teens, lean and sunburnt from picking cotton. Perhaps she would have gone with the other farm workers taking a luxurious Saturday night off.

Bailey's closest traveling companion was usually Uncle Dave Macon. If a hotel refused to allow Bailey inside, Uncle Dave insisted that Bailey was his valet. Roy Acuff also made a point of having Bailey with him when he toured. Acuff, destined to become synonymous with the Opry in the coming decades, was still unknown in the 1930s. He knew that if he brought along the Opry's Harmonica Wizard, he'd fill the house. Bailey told his biographers that Bill Monroe, the Father of Bluegrass, paid him well and made sure that he got whatever he wanted to eat from restaurants.

However, the Opry's early tours were not entirely utopic visions of enlightened artists aiding each other. Bailey navigated a narrow racial space with a set of complex, unspoken rules. For example, The Delmore Brothers, a popular act whose personal character Bailey always praised, would refuse to eat in a restaurant that wouldn't serve Bailey, but they also included a blackface routine in their act. Humphrey Bate, the distinguished physician who had insisted that Judge Hay audition Bailey in 1925, included a song called "Run, Nigger, Run" in his repertoire.

Bailey was popular with his fans and his fellow performers. He was well-liked and talented. But he had begun his career performing in the corner of a dining room and he never fully escaped that corner. He told his biographers that, when he was backstage, he made it a point never to speak unless spoken to. On the road, he often slept in the car or with a local black family who would take him in. On the Opry, he was strictly a solo performer and never allowed to join the spontaneous jams which often broke out. Although he was also a talented guitar player and vocalist, Bailey was not allowed to sing or speak into the microphone; Judge Hay was afraid whites would stop listening if too many realized the Harmonica Wizard was black. By the end of the 1930s, musical tastes were changing; Bailey's corner was getting smaller, and there was nothing he could do to keep his career alive.

Before the decade was out, WSM became financially independent of National Life and the Opry became more polished. The Opry didn't need to sell life insurance any more. It just needed to provide an outlet for popular music, and that, too, was changing. Harmonica solos, an integral part of the old-time, blues-inflected sound of rural music in the early 20th century, were being phased out in favor of more elaborate bands. As a result, blues and country were beginning to travel more distinct paths. Bailey wanted to adapt to the new styles, but was told not to. He told Morton that he came in one day practicing a modern pop hit, "Blue Heaven," but was ordered not to play it on the air. He was expected to stick to bluesy tunes.

By the end of the 1930s, each musician on the Opry played in standard "slots." Bailey's time slot was just after the Fruit Jar Drinkers and just before the crooning tones of Ford Rush. The little man who had dominated the Opry playlist in the 1920s and filled concert halls in the early 1930s would often come to the Opry and stand around backstage all night, waiting to play a couple songs.

In early 1941, the American Society of Composers, Authors, and Publishers (ASCAP), which owned the rights to the songs of nearly all the musicians on the Opry, announced that it would be doubling its fees.

In response, WSM sent an edict to all its artists: *Stop playing your ASCAP songs*. Nearly every song in Bailey's 60-tune repertoire had an ASCAP copyright, even the ones he'd known since childhood. Limited for so long, he told Morton that he couldn't adapt to the new edict quickly enough. So in May 1941, George Hay fired DeFord Bailey from the Grand Ole Opry. Hay tells it like this in his 1945 self-published book *A History of the Grand Ole Opry*:

That brings us to DeFord Bailey, a little crippled colored boy who was a bright feature of our show for about 15 years. Like some members of his race and other races, he was lazy. He knew about a dozen numbers … but he refused to learn any more … He was our mascot and is still loved by the entire company … When we were forced to give him his final notice, DeFord said without malice: "I knowed it wuz comin', Judge, I knowed it wuz comin.'"

For decades, this was considered the true story of the end of Bailey's career. Roy Acuff, probably believing that he was exonerating Bailey in an article written upon his death, told *The Tennessean*, "It wasn't that he wouldn't learn any new tunes, he *couldn't* learn any new tunes." But this isn't true either. Bailey had, after all, learned to imitate barnyard animals on a harmonica when he was three and was clearly a versatile, gifted musician. Sitting in that high-rise public housing unit 30 years after losing his job with the Opry, Bailey recalled a different version of the events to Morton: WSM used him to make their money, then, "They turned me loose to root, hog, or die."

### THE BLUES FESTIVAL, 2006

At nine p.m. on a Saturday in June, I found myself walking in a place that every iota of my white suburban existence had conditioned me to avoid—down Jefferson Street, alone, in the dark. Well, I wasn't really alone: somewhere off in the distance there were 20,000 people enjoying a jazz and blues festival. Since I was arriving late, I passed only rows of parked cars and the occasional pedestrian heading home early. The streetlights were dim, but I knew my skin glowed conspicuously. Everybody I passed nodded or smiled and I wondered, unable to stop myself, "Am I just another person going to a music festival, or am I a white person going to a jazz and blues festival on Jefferson Street?"

From the 1920s until it was split by I-40 in the 1960s, Jefferson Street was the heart of Nashville's African-American community, lined with shops, theatres, night clubs, and restaurants, and not far from Fisk University. In the '40s, '50s, and early '60s, Jeff Street also became the center of the national R&B scene. A slew of clubs—the Del Morocco, the New Era, Sugar Hill, Ebony Circle, the Baron—were devoted to the music. A local radio station, WLAC, broadcast R&B across the country while other stations still considered the music taboo. WLAC-TV's "Night Train" debuted in 1964, predating Chicago's famous "Soul Train" by five years.

By the time Nashville's R&B scene was jumping, DeFord Bailey was back to shining shoes in his downtown shop. He played his harp for his customers, but never returned to the stage professionally. His eldest son, DeFord Bailey, Jr., learned to play the guitar and became a popular bluesman down on Jeff Street. DeFord, Jr. rubbed shoulders with other up-and-comers like Little Richard, and performed at clubs frequented by Joe Louis and Roy Campanella on their trips through Nashville. DeFord, Jr. also made friends with another new guitarist on the scene. Nicknamed "Marbles," this young man was a regular at the Del Morocco and regarded as something of an oddity; he occasionally played the guitar with his teeth. DeFord, Jr. liked him and often invited him over for dinner at his parents' house. I imagine plates of mashed potatoes and meatloaf passed around the table and wonder exactly what DeFord Bailey and Jimi Hendrix talked about. Music, no doubt.

I never really got into the blues myself, raised as I was on country, folk, and Big Band. But I'd discovered be-bop jazz—Coltrane, Davis, and the like—in college and recently rekindled my interest in the genre, so the "Jazz" half of the "Jefferson Street Jazz and Blues Festival" sounded appealing. The evening's final act was billed as a "Tribute to DeFord Bailey." Amid all the other summer festivals in the area that week—The CMA Fan Fest, Bonnaroo, and the R.C. and Moon Pie Festival—the local paper had hardly mentioned this Jefferson Street Jazz and Blues festival. I suppose I pictured it as a slightly more intimate gathering of jazz aficionados listening carefully to each song and muttering their opinions to each other beneath the applause. Instead, I found a massive crowd of people that seemed to stretch for blocks in front of the stage.

This was the Blues. The Blues with a capital B. Perhaps I'd never appreciated the genre because I'd never seen it live before. I bought a can of warm Coke and squeezed into the crowd right on the line between the people who were dancing and the people who were watching. I assumed, at first, my reporter's pose, standing erect with an open notebook and poised pen while Nick Nixon and the Jefferson Street All Star Band riffed through "Mustang Sally" and "Sweet Home Chicago." Then Nixon invited Marion James, "Nashville's Queen of the Blues" onstage and I turned to see an elderly woman, assisted by two men, grabbing the handrail and climbing the stairs tentatively. I expected a short speech and some applause, but James stepped up to the microphone and was transformed. "My Baby Don't Stand No Cheatin'"—she belted it out until I thought the pavement would buckle, until I thought the entire world was made up of nothing but this woman's voice and the bass guitar and brass behind her. When she finished, the men reappeared, took her elbows, and gingerly escorted her back off the stage.

After James, Johnny "Guitar" Jones took the stage. "Nashville used to be Country Music, U.S.A.," he yelled to the crowd, "but then we brought the blues up here and it became Music City, U.S.A." The crowd yelled and clapped. I stood and marveled at this music, the soundtrack to another entire set of lives, unfolding around me. I thought about Joey and my black friends in high school, how comfortable they would probably be if they were here, as comfortable as my white friends and I had been at the Ryman, or the Bluebird, or trading the latest Flecktones CD around during lunch. I wasn't the only white face on Jeff Street that night, but I could pick out each one. There were no more than half a dozen of us. How had music become so segregated in Music City, U.S.A.? And how was it that R&B had been erased from the city's official history, that a festival which attracted 20,000 people and several blues legends had received only a six-inch article in the Local/State section of *The Tennessean*?

At 10 p.m., the headline act took the stage. It was Herschel Bailey, DeFord Sr.'s grandson. "Let's hear it for my grandfather, DeFord Bailey," he yelled. The crowd roared. When they settled, he said, "Finally elected to the Country Music Hall of Fame after all these years." I expected a more tepid reaction from the crowd. After all, hadn't the African-Americans' share of country music's heritage been wrestled away from them? But the crowd roared even louder, and Herschel invited his father, DeFord, Jr., to the stage. Both men were dressed as Bailey Sr. liked to dress—sharp. They wore fedoras and their clothing had creases you could slice bread with. DeFord, Jr. wore a white suit and shiny tan shoes. Herschel, a loose orange dress shirt and gold chain. DeFord, Jr. picked up the bass and Herschel sang "We Gonna Have a Funky Good Time." After the song ended, I rushed backstage to shake DeFord, Jr.'s hand and my musical path, at last, converged with the Baileys for just a moment.

Onstage, Herschel was riffing on OutKast's "I Like the Way You Move." The dancers in the crowd formed distinct lines and columns and began a synchronized dance that resembled line dancing. As much as it looked like The Electric Slide, someone called it the "Mississippi Swing" and someone else referred to it as "twining." I tried joining in, but I was pathetic, single-handedly verifying every stereotype about white people and rhythm. I couldn't master the quarter turns and the slides. I stepped on feet and ran into people. Some dancers tried to help me. "Turn!" they yelled. "Slide!" "Left!" Right!" They were smiling and I was smiling, but I soon decided to sit down and get out of the way.

I would love to say that the dancers beckoned me back but they didn't. Some spectators cleared a spot for me and I sat on the asphalt, aware, suddenly, of everything around me—the smell of hot chicken stands, the warm pavement beneath me, Herschel's voice, Reeboks and FILAs and leather sandals dancing in front of me. Past the crowd, I saw DeFord, Jr. standing by his car just off the cloverleaf. Music in Nashville, I realized, is also an artery of sorts, circulating fluidly through the city, keeping it fresh and vibrant even when we're not giving it the attention we should. I watched Deford, Jr. watching his son and wondered where, next, the music would take us.

# 17TH AND JO JOHNSTON

### THIS WAS ONCE AN ALL-BLACK SCHOOL, NOVEMBER 1990

I walked out the gym door in shorts, carrying my blue hoodie, and saw my father through the dusk over by the main doors. It was, of course, a major *faux pas* for parents to actually get out of the car when they came to pick up their children. Most of us seventh-graders, with our social status still in flux, had been busy cultivating the impression that we'd hatched from eggs and raised ourselves. I crossed the long school yard, aware as I walked of the sweat drying along my hairline, of my stork legs, and how my father, standing there with his head back and mouth slightly agape, looked like a fish with a mustache.

"Dad," I said, slinking over to him. I hadn't bothered with the locker room after tryouts, just walked outside in my sweaty clothes. I had a couple of minutes to hustle Dad to the car before the other girls came out. He was admiring the architecture, taking in the granite façade. There was a steel clock above the front entryway, *Pearl High School* carved beneath it in Art-Deco letters.

"I just had to see this building up close. Put your sweatshirt on," he said without looking away. I pulled the hoodie over my head. My school did look kind of cool from that angle. The granite contrasted with the brick, the white-framed windows, and the gathering November darkness.

In seventh grade, my sense of purpose was elusive at best, but the building where I attended classes seemed stately and proud as I gazed up at it.

"You know, Erin," Dad said, "It's really a privilege to go here."

I knew he wasn't referring to my school in its incarnation as MLK Magnet but to its past as Pearl High. Even today, a quarter-century after Pearl's African-American student body was bused to another high school and Pearl High ceased to be, it's still considered a cornerstone of Nashville's black community. As proud as my parents were when I was accepted to MLK, my dad was especially excited that his daughter would be going to a school with such a venerable past. I didn't really care, myself. For me, MLK was a chance to escape my neighborhood school and all the classmates who'd pegged me as a geek and an outcast. Besides, in sixth-grade Social Studies at my old school, we'd learned about *Brown vs. the Board of Education*, that the Supreme Court had ruled separate-but-equal schools unconstitutional in 1954. I figured Pearl had not been all-black for decades. A bunch of people who had attended Pearl 40 years before me could not have seemed less relevant to seventh grade, to everything I hoped would happen.

"I don't think I made the team," I said.

"Oh?"

"The other girls made fun of the way I shoot. Coach didn't tell them to stop."

We talked about the possibility of playing basketball in a rec league for a moment before Dad finally looked away from the building, put his hand on my shoulder, and steered me toward the car. At the community center and park across the street, bluish white streetlights buzzed and came to life. The housing projects, catty-corner from the school, seemed cast in shadow. A few yellowing lights flickered weakly. Dad, who is a city planner, has often told me how easy it is to spot the poor, mostly black neighborhoods from an airplane above any major city at night. Public works employees don't check the light bulbs much in those parts of town. All you have to do, he says, is look for the darkest areas.

"Your mother said to bring home Wendy's for supper. Sound good?"

I looked out across the neighborhood. It seemed alien enough in the daylight. In the dark, it was foreboding and scary. I wanted to be home, where I didn't have to think about school, or basketball, or whether or not I would ever fit in anywhere.

"Yeah, let's get out of here."

MLK, or King, was verbal shorthand for my school's absurdly long name: Martin Luther King, Jr. Magnet High School for the Health Sciences and Engineering. In sixth grade, when my parents received a letter saying I'd qualified for the lottery for MLK's entering class, I held the accompanying brochure with the same reverence I would later reserve for concert tickets. The school's full name, written in a dignified all-capital font, took up three entire lines across the front. I remember opening the brochure carefully, reading about the school's new Technology Lab and its selection of honors classes. I had plans for this school—it would the a place where I belonged. After I was accepted, Mom, Dad, Cathleen, and I celebrated with a milkshake at Dalt's Grille.

Magnet schools, as the name suggests, pulled students from all over the city. In my part of town, where my friends and I had started talking about possible colleges over our lunches in the fifth grade, they were a very big deal. I remember the smartest kid in my class thoughtfully waving a half-eaten French fry as he opined, "Magnet schools are ideal because you get the same education as at a private school, but they're *way* more diverse than the private schools. Colleges like that." However, the schools had one major drawback for Green Hills whites hoping to get their children prepped for college. I learned this the day I failed to get into Meigs, the middle school magnet. My friend's mother told me, "It's okay, Erin. Did you know they found a body on the front lawn at Meigs one morning last year?" She nodded and raised her eyebrows. "It's in a *very* bad part of town."

All three of the magnet schools were near, or in, downtown Nashville. When I was growing up, no one ever said "inner city." During middle school, I'd spent a day at MLK as a contestant in the Metro Science Fair. The fair was on a Saturday and my mother was going to drive my friend and me to the school to set up our project displays that morning. We'd have some time to kill while the projects were being judged.

"We could go to Fountain Square," my friend said to me in the cafeteria the day before the fair. Fountain Square was a new, urban mall. "It's nearby. Your mom could drive us."

"Is it close enough to walk?" I asked.

"Well, it might be. But you know, MLK is in a *black neighborhood*."

That was our term, and it meant nearly everything that race meant to middle-class whites in the '80s and '90s. Black neighborhood meant you could probably walk around, in daylight at least, but was it worth the risk? Of course, there are plenty of nice people living there, but you just don't know what might happen, sticking out as you would. Black neighborhood meant you locked the car doors. It meant grocery stores with bars on the windows and blocks of identical government-housing units. It meant walking between your parents when you left the Nashville Sounds' ballpark after a game. Those two words said all those things.

My mother drove us to Fountain Square that Saturday.

## OLD PEARL

After I stood with my father outside the school that November evening, I occasionally tried to imagine Pearl students walking alongside me down the long, brick-paved hallways—faint outlines in long skirts and letter sweaters. I wondered what their lives had been like, what they had hoped for. Their apparitions seemed distant, dusty, and ancient, but I could just as well have pictured those former students with Afro picks and tight jeans. Pearl was a completely black school until 1971, when court-ordered busing forced its integration. Most of the whites subsequently zoned for Pearl in the 1970s simply refused to go there, claiming that the school had inadequate facilities and poor academic standards. The school board closed Pearl in 1983, the same year I began kindergarten at a public school down the street from my house. Three years later, MLK Magnet was created, giving students from all over the city the chance to take honors classes, win national science fairs, and get into pre-med programs. We had no idea that kids from the area had lost their neighborhood school. We certainly had no understanding of the community that had built Pearl to begin with.

---

Nashville's black community gathered strength immediately after the Civil War. Nearby, Atlanta was pulling itself from the rubble left in Sherman's wake, but Nashville's infrastructure was still intact. Ex-slaves flocked to the city to receive rations, medical care, and education from the Freedman's Bureau. In 1866, white northerners built Fisk University for blacks. Meharry Medical School followed in 1876. Both of these institutions still educate in the heart of North Nashville, within sight of the top-floor windows at MLK.

Pearl, named for a Union sympathizer and Nashville's first school superintendent, was the only public school for blacks in Nashville when it opened in 1883. It served students from first to eighth grade.

Through the 1880s, the effort to establish an actual high school was spearheaded by James Napier, an attorney and the last black councilman the city would have until the 1940s. Napier led mass meetings at Clark Chapel Methodist Episcopal Church, where activists drew up a petition demanding that the school board establish a high school for African-Americans. The board relented in 1886, but the resulting school only went up to the 11th grade. It was another decade before any black in the city could get a high school diploma.

Finally, in 1897, a 12th grade was established. The first blacks in Nashville to earn their high school diplomas graduated in 1898. With the educational opportunities provided by a high school, three colleges, and a medical school within a four-mile radius, Nashville's black community was a vibrant city within a city. A comfortable middle class thrived, centered on the North Nashville neighborhood near Pearl, with more black businessmen, lawyers, physicians, and politicians than any comparable city in the South.

For decades after Reconstruction, many local governments in Tennessee offered high school courses and graduation credits to whites only. I have interviewed rural African-Americans who lived with relatives in Nashville while they earned their diplomas at Pearl during the 1920s. Obviously, this presented major challenges to blacks hoping to obtain an education. In 1930, fewer than 900 blacks in the entire state had graduated from high school. Most blacks in Tennessee were domestic or menial workers. But Pearl High School continued to grow, burgeoned as it was by hopes for something better.

By the early '30s, the little building it leased on the Fisk campus had become too crowded. A new building, designed by McKissack and McKissack, an all-black architectural firm, and built entirely by black contractors and masons, opened for classes in the fall of 1936. Pearl's new campus took up about six acres in the middle of an ethnically diverse neighborhood of modest, well-kept wood-frame houses, shops, and restaurants. The big hangout for the Pearl kids was a Greek eatery nearby. The school's front doors faced 17th Avenue and a sprawling, whites-only park, shaded by towering magnolias and dotted with picnic benches and tennis courts. Another side of the campus bordered the L&N railroad tracks, with Fisk just beyond.

Inside, the new Pearl High had room for over 1,000 students and was considered one of the finest black high school facilities in the nation. It had one of the first gymnatoriums in the city, a music room with built-in risers and adjoining practice rooms, spacious classrooms and science labs, and windows that stretched from the tops of the radiators to the ceiling. Fifty-four years after classes began in the building, I walked into that worn but still immaculate space to begin my career as a student at Martin Luther King Magnet School.

## WAKING UP, SEPTEMBER 1990

MLK fell short of my expectations almost immediately. Really, there's no way it could have met them since I was hoping for a hybrid between Encore (an elementary school enrichment program where we'd conducted an archeological dig behind the school for history class) and that episode of *The Simpsons* where Bart cheats his way into a school for gifted students. "We have only one rule here," Bart's new teacher told him. "*Make your own rules!*" I'd anticipated an academic and social utopia—a geek paradise where I could be the cool kid. What I found was junior high.

At MLK, everyone was trying to scramble out of the niche they'd held in middle school and take control of their own social destinies. It was, at least, more diverse than our zoned schools. I had more black acquaintances than I would've had otherwise, a Laotian friend, and an ongoing flirtation with a Kurdish boy—but when it came to finding a clique, most stuck with their own race. After a couple weeks in the scrum, including an incident where I sat down at the popular kids' lunch table and they all moved, I found my gang. These were the girls who read Christopher Pike during lunch and wore bright cotton print shirts. Non-threatening. I struck my new friends as pleasantly odd (kind of a cross between a hippie and a nerd, my still-best-friend, Paula, recently told me), and they appreciated my ability to quote Monty Python at length.

I accepted my place, happy to at least fit in somewhere, but it rankled that I couldn't shake my outsider status even at a science magnet school. At lunch, my gang and I were relegated to the perimeter, far from the social epicenter of the cafeteria. While my friends debated the merits of *Flowers in the Attic*, I watched the crowd surging around the popular table. The dominant junior high clique was white and athletic. They never seemed to eat during lunch; they just laughed. I wanted, just once, to know what was so funny.

I also learned in seventh grade that adults have all the power, even if they're wrong. I was introduced to higher-level English by a teacher who dictated the number of sentences we were to include in a paragraph, and counted points off my sentence diagrams because my lines slanted the wrong direction. Our band director had us playing Barry Manilow tunes in front of the school. Students who made the honor roll had to march in front of a school assembly, one by one, every six weeks, to pick up a certificate and a Blow-Pop. None of this seemed like a good idea to me, but it didn't matter. Our guidance counselor had a poster in her office that said it all: *Teenagers, quick! Move out, get a job, while you still know everything.* Adults didn't take us seriously.

---

  I did enjoy the car rides to school. On the frequent mornings when I'd forced my mother to wait at the bottom of the stairs, briefcase in hand, calling my name, I ate cereal from a Tupperware bowl for the first few minutes of the drive while Mom vented. During this part of the car ride, we were still in our corner of town, cruising down Granny White Pike, passing one wide green yard after another, each occupied by a rancher set far back from the road. We passed my old Montessori preschool, then a private Church of Christ school, and then Moore, the junior high I was zoned for. Despite my tribulations at MLK, I always felt a surge of gratitude when we drove by Moore. Built in the 1970s, there was nothing attractive about that building—one-story, shaped like an H, the dull brown brick punctuated by tinted windows. When Mom was really angry, she'd threaten to fill out transfer forms. "You could be riding the bus to Moore *tomorrow*, do you understand me?" Fortunately, Mom inevitably cooled off. I'd make an earnest though fruitless promise not to make her late any more and the conversation would shift to music, church, or current events.

  My favorite part of the drive was Music Row, a tree-lined neighborhood of record companies, recording studios, and old houses that had been converted to offices for songwriting groups. Whenever a member scored a big hit, the office would hang a banner outside: "Congratulations DeWayne Blackwell for 'Friends in Low Places,' Number 1!" for instance. I kept an eye out for new ones. By the end of seventh grade, I'd started writing songs in my class notebooks. By the end of eighth grade, my identity as a writer was firmly cemented in the minds of my teachers and peers. I loved those banners, because they reminded me that my dreams, constantly changing though they were, might be as close to realization as a few verses penciled in the margin of my Algebra notes.

  Music Row ended at the Country Music Hall of Fame. Two blocks later, we crossed Church Street and the cityscape changed again. Here, we passed the liquor store, the undertakers' school, and the plasma donation center, and my mood often soured. The bleakness reminded me that it was only 7:20 in the morning. I knew that the radio-listening and conversation with my mother, who allowed me to flip incessantly between the three stations that might play a Beatles song, would soon end, and I'd be faced with an entire day of school. The John Henry Hale housing projects began as soon as we crossed Charlotte Avenue—duplex after duplex with concrete stoops, brown screen doors, and T-shaped iron clothesline poles. Their rows created tunnels and I craned my head as they flashed by, trying to catch a glimpse of life in the projects.

In school I was always near a window, watching people come and go from the neighborhood. I think I was searching for anything that could affirm that I deserved to live in Green Hills and the people in the projects deserved to live there. I'd seen enough of the evening news to know that Nashville's housing projects were drug-infested and crime-ridden, but whenever I looked, I only saw people sitting on their stoops talking, kids on push toys, laundry catching the breeze. Once I was back in Green Hills with my friends, I joked about drive-by shooting drills, a popular magnet school myth.

Mornings when Mom dropped me off, lines of elementary school kids waited for the bus under the watch of a few neighborhood mothers. My mom pulled over at the corner of 17th and Jo Johnston, right in front of the projects, and unlocked the car doors. If there was a red light and I had time, I groused about 7:30 being an inhumane hour for English.

"Erin, look at those kids lined up there," Mom would say. There must have been about 30 of them every morning, roughhousing and chattering, carrying disproportionately large backpacks. "Their schools don't start for another hour and a half, but they're already out here waiting for the bus."

This did seem unjust. I'd gone to an elementary school just a mile from my house. Where were *their* neighborhood schools? I could never figure it out, even felt a pang of guilt when I passed them, but I was too stubborn to reveal my true feelings on the matter to my mom.

"Whatever. They're six, they don't know what time it is." And with that, I'd climb out, grab my saxophone, lunchbox, and backpack, and sprint through the intersection, past the little church and the beauty salon, across the school yard, up the stairs, and through the doorway under the steel clock.

# COMPROMISE

When I started seventh grade, over a third of the students at King were black. Most of us at the school genuinely appreciated its diversity and the chance to get to know one another, although it in no way resembled the smiling, flag-waving propaganda we'd seen on all the elementary school bulletin boards. I was learning, awkwardly, that race was more than skin color, that my identity was bound up in there somewhere. Quite suddenly during a Black History Month assembly, my white friends and I also realized that many of our black peers were angry. A bespectacled, popular high-school boy with skin the color of cocoa gave a speech honoring the African-American call-and-response tradition. "Angel's Food Cake is white, and Devil's Food Cake is black," he cried, "In our society, white is called good and black is synonymous with evil. What are we, as black children, supposed to do with that imagery? How are we supposed to see ourselves?"

"Amen!" the crowd roared while I sank in my seat.

"Now, let us all stand for the Black National Anthem, 'Lift Ev'ry Voice and Sing,'" the boy said. A senior with a strong soprano came to the microphone. As she sang, the black kids chorused in and the vibrato sound of it all filled the gymnatorium. Powerful as it was, I couldn't do much but fiddle with the hem of my t-shirt and look around. I'd never heard the song before. After school that day, while waiting for the city bus, my white friends and I sat in the school yard, facing the projects, and wondered what "they" had been so mad about in assembly. The answer, or at least part of it, was right under my nose, especially when I ran past the crowd of elementary school children waiting for their bus each morning.

Those kids weren't going to nearby schools because Nashville's busing-for-racial-balance plan mandated that elementary students travel out of the city to attend schools in predominantly white neighborhoods. Busing had been implemented in Nashville at the start of the 1971-72 school year. The initial plan moved equal percentages of blacks and whites around the county, but whites were the dominant protestors. They spoke, not only in picket lines, but with their attendance. Citing "safety concerns," whites pulled their children out of public schools at an alarming rate and sent them to private, religiously-affiliated schools; many had been built expressly to accommodate them. Throughout the 1970s, school officials scrambled to re-draw the zoning lines in an effort to maintain racial balance at the schools. As they searched for compromises to keep whites enrolled in the public school system, talk of closing Pearl began.

The school board decided that students in grades one to four would be bused to schools along the city's outer edge, then bused into the city for grades five and six. Some high schools would close and others would be expanded into Comprehensive High Schools, which would offer both vo-tech and college preparatory classes, as well as a vast array of sports and activities. To provide so many options, they would need a lot of land, and to get that kind of land, the comprehensive schools would need to be in suburban areas. So African-Americans would be bused out to the perimeter of the city once again. Magnet schools were also part of the master plan. They would attract high-achieving students to inner-city schools, balancing the movement of black and white students through the city each day, theoretically making it fair.

By 1986, kids like me were going to Pearl. The historically black elementary and junior high schools, which the children waiting for the bus on the corner might have attended, were razed to build Pearl-Cohn Comprehensive High School, the only inner city high school in Nashville. The other half of the school's name came from Cohn High, a predominantly white school whose attendance had dropped precipitously when busing began. Children from the housing projects did get to attend a school just down the road for fifth and sixth grade. For those two years, they could walk while whites were bused in. Sitting on the lawn at King after school, we watched them pass.

The extent of the whites' busing burden, our big compromise, was coming into the projects everyday to take college prep courses. We felt brave and exotic, because we took hard classes and rode the city buses home everyday. We had no idea that students had been coming from all over to get a first-class education in that building for over a century. "People walked to Pearl," Ted Lenox, a 1943 graduate told me. "They came from across the Cumberland River, from all over town."

In the 1940s and '50s, Pearl offered an array of classes—drama, music, Latin, French and Spanish. Vo-tech students could learn carpentry, tailoring, and masonry. The school had its own swing band for dances in the gym. On those nights, they called the gym the Cotton Club, after the famous joint in Harlem where blacks were allowed to perform but not dance. Teachers were strict and encouraging even though they only had second-hand textbooks, made much less money than their white counterparts, and knew that professional opportunities for graduates were slim. "Where the blacks are now, they couldn't get there then," Mr. Lenox said. "Doctors, lawyers, teachers, that was about all you saw back then."

But a black child in Nashville could complete his or her entire education, from elementary to post-graduate, within a two-mile radius. It was an exceptional education, too. Academically, Pearl was consistently trading places with Dunbar High in Washington, D.C. as the top-ranked black school in the nation. It also excelled athletically. The basketball team won several national black high school tournaments. In 1966, when the Tennessee State Championship was first integrated, Pearl won handily.

Mr. Lenox, who played basketball in the '40s, is now the school historian, running a small museum in what used to be the home team's locker room. When I phoned his house one Sunday evening, I had just missed a gathering of Pearl graduates from the early 1940s. They meet once a month. This is not uncommon among Pearl alums. On any given weekend in Nashville, Pearl alumni are getting together at someone's home. Once a month, they meet in a large group at the Shoney's near the Titans' stadium. They sing their Alma Mater at the close of each meeting.

I don't know my Alma Mater.

## DEVIANCE AND DEMOCRACY, OCTOBER 1991

The craftsmen who built Pearl High laid a tile compass into the floor just inside the entryway. It was done in green and brown hues with an arrow fixed at north. Sometimes, when no one was looking, I'd stand on it facing northwest, looking roughly toward my friend who'd moved to Canada. Sometimes I'd face southwest, which would take me through Green Hills and home. It always seemed appropriate to me, even at the time, that I crossed a compass each morning on the way to class, because along with being a geek, I was a wanderer.

Wandering served me. In junior high, I felt restless, disjointed, happy only when I was looking out a window or in motion. I had a keen sense of the injustices I believed were heaped upon me, of my lack of power. I wandered to ease frustrations, burn energy. Sometimes it calmed me. Sometimes it got me out of things I didn't want to do.

In eighth grade, I was in the school band, but budget cuts meant we only had practice twice a week. For one term, I was assigned to P.E. for the other three days, but when the teacher spent nearly the entire first day explaining precisely what color qualified as Royal Blue, I knew I had to get out of there. So my band friends and I explained to Coach

Jackson that band was five days a week and never went back. Instead, we explored. Even though the facility was well past its prime, with peeling paint and hissing water pipes, we could see hints of its former glory. It was massive. MLK's student body barely filled half the building. Old wooden desks were stacked in the shadowy Vo-Tech wing, but we found what must have been a cosmetology classroom and the concrete bays for auto repair, where sunlight streamed into the garage windows and cut through clouds of dust.

At lunch, in every season, my friends and I ate quickly, walked outside to the old football field, and paced along the wooden bleachers, talking. MLK did not have a football team and the field had fallen into disrepair. Sometimes, smoke from the foundry across the tracks cloaked us in acrid fog. The bleachers were warped and creaky, completely devoid of paint. Sometimes boards shifted or broke as we walked over them. The press box hadn't been painted in our school's colors yet (blue, white, and yellow). Instead, it was covered by weathered, chipping coats of red and white, Pearl's colors. Its floor was covered in dirt, leaves, and trash.

During one lunch walk, the hot topic was SQ5R, a mandatory note-taking style enforced by our U.S. History teacher. SQ5R involved alternating columns of questions and responses. I could never figure out what kind of an idiot would write down questions in class notes when it was hard enough to keep up with the answers. Still, Mrs. Braun collected and graded our notes once a week, and I was doing poorly in the class as a result. Since we were, after all, learning about democracy in class, we decided to circulate a petition demanding the termination of SQ5R.

It made the rounds during eighth-grade lunch and amazingly, for our little peripheral group, collected 75 signatures. For once, the biggest crowd in the cafeteria was around *our* table. "Now we need one of those introductory paragraphs to explain our case," someone behind me said as I admired the petition, which was heavy with erasable Bic ink. Everyone looked at me. I skipped my daily bleacher walk to sit in the cafeteria, which always smelled like old shoes and bleach, and wrote what I referred to as a Preamble. Then, one of the stealthier kids slid the petition and my Preamble into Mrs. Braun's mailbox in the main office.

The next morning, we were working silently in our vocabulary books in English class when the teacher approached me from behind, leaning around to look me in the eye in that way that teachers do. "Erin," she whispered, "We read your Preamble in the teacher's lounge this morning."

My heart lurched. They had noticed! Was I about to get in trouble for taking a stand? Or would she sympathize with our cause?

"You should be a comedian," she said, smiling, giving me a pat on the shoulder, and walking away.

### WE WENT ON LIKE IT WOULD LAST FOREVER

As I've researched Pearl, I've been amazed at all the places I've found alumni. I set out looking for two: Mr. Lenox, and Rip Patton, class of 1958. I'd heard Mr. Patton mention Pearl during a lecture about his experiences as a Freedom Rider and subsequent four-month stint in the Parchman Penitentiary.

Then, searching Nashville for an expert on the city's civil rights movement, I found Linda Wynn, class of 1966, now a lecturer at Fisk. Ms. Wynn gave me some dates to investigate in *The Nashville Tennessean's* archives. I put a call in to their archivist and prepared to wait. *The Tennessean* is the only newspaper in town now, and there's only one librarian to handle all the requests for faxes and reprints. Generally, it takes about a week to hear back from her, so I was surprised when the newspaper's phone number showed up on my caller ID before I'd had my coffee the next morning.

"Do you still need information on Old Pearl?" Chantay Steptoe, the head librarian asked me.

I said I did. "Oh, good," she said. "Listen, I can help you with anything you need." I thanked her. She added, "I only ask that you let me have a copy of your essay."

My decaffeinated mind finally forged a connection. "Ms. Steptoe, are you a Pearl alum?"

"Yes, I am! Class of 1978!"

So I told her I was looking for articles about the board's decision to close the school. From reading *The Burden of Busing* by Richard Pride and David Woodard, the only book that extensively analyzes Nashville's busing struggle, I knew that the community had rallied to save Pearl in the late '70s, but they had been overruled in the '80s. Ms. Steptoe called me back the next day with some articles she was going to fax, but she cautioned me. "This isn't quite what you're looking for. No one really reported on Pearl at the time. Everything that was done, well, it was kept pretty quiet." She was right. The fax contained articles with headlines like "The Pearl-Cohn Melting Pot." There was one article, written weeks after Pearl had been shut down, that hinted at the anger and frustration. The headline quoted Pearl's white principal:

"'Pearl High School made court-ordered changes work,' ex-official says." I called Ms. Steptoe back and asked her if they'd believed Pearl would close when she was a teenager.

"Oh, no. We went on like it would last forever, just like it always had."

What I know from my research is that the black community felt set upon. Blacks wanted integration and equality, not forced assimilation. Pride and Woodard quote one frustrated black leader at the time, who asked, "Why give white children the concept that what's good is only good in their part of town?" Under the 1971-72 busing plan, Pearl was projected to have 908 whites and 565 blacks, but only 350 whites showed up on the first day of classes. By 1978, when Ms. Steptoe was a senior, fewer than 100 whites attended Pearl. The rest of the whites zoned for Pearl moved, enrolled in private schools, or received academic transfers from the school board.

The problems that whites had with Pearl were bound up in both race and symbolism. They were more than willing to transfer to a comprehensive school like Hillsboro, which also had a formidable number of black students. But with Pearl, it was a matter of principle. Pride writes, "For whites, to go to Pearl was to acknowledge that black culture—its values, traditions, and institutions—was on par with white culture .... For them, Pearl, North Nashville, and the black culture together represented crime, violence, welfare, pregnancy, poverty, and anti-white sentiment."

"They were a little afraid," Ms. Steptoe said of the few white teenagers who went to school with her. "All we knew was, 'Man, they're going to be sending more white people.' But the ones who stuck it out, I think everything worked out for them."

The school board's academic transfer policy particularly infuriated leaders working to save Pearl. Pride writes, "They saw it as a willingness on the part of school officials to undermine the school, the black community, and desegregation." Board officials were approving more than 80% of the transfer requests that crossed their desks. Pearl was nearly closed after the 1977-78 school year, but the black community mobilized once again. Leaders and black school board members demanded that courses offered at the comprehensive schools be offered at Pearl as well. In 1979, the school board agreed to offer four such courses at Pearl. By October, only four of the 57 students who had requested those classes actually enrolled in them. Pearl's final school year was 1982-83, a century after Nashville's blacks had first organized to demand their right to a high school diploma. Only 19 white students remained at Pearl.

## THIS WAS ONCE MY SCHOOL, 2006

I applied to Hume-Fogg, the other magnet high school, in eighth grade, but was put on the waiting list. When my number came up the summer before 10th grade, I decided to go. This was mainly a pragmatic decision. If I'd stayed at King, I would have been required to take an AP science class. By the time I was 14, the idea that I would pursue advanced study in biology, physics, or chemistry was laughable.

If I had known my history better when I was 15, I would have known that Hume-Fogg's discarded books were subsequently used at Pearl while the schools were segregated. I didn't know that, but I did know that going to Hume-Fogg would allow me to take creative writing from Bill Brown, a poet who had just won a national award for teaching. I knew Hume-Fogg was in the heart of downtown Nashville, not far from the Ryman Auditorium. And in Green Hills, whenever I uttered the phrase, "I go to a magnet school," in cursory small-talk, the other person in the conversation usually said, "Hume-Fogg?" And when I said, "No, MLK," their response invariably was, "Now, where is that exactly?" You could walk from one to the other, but they were worlds apart, as they had been for over a century. In a decision I sometimes regret today, the tipping point for my decision was that my neighbors held Hume-Fogg in higher esteem.

In 1995, just before my senior year, a family from Green Hills sued Metro-Nashville Public Schools because their daughter had not been selected for Hume-Fogg. An investigation revealed that the magnet school lotteries were, in fact, not random, but determined by an algorithm based on the letters of a student's last name. As the school board worked on revamping the system, and preventing future lawsuits, they decided to do away with affirmative action. Separate lotteries for whites and blacks were eliminated. Today, MLK has over 1,100 students, twice as many as it did when I was in seventh grade, but blacks make up a far lower percentage of the total student population. When I attended MLK, part of its appeal was that I was as likely to see a black face as a white one in the hallway. Now, African Americans are the clear minority, just as they are in most high schools in the county.

Nashville's blacks have struggled for parity with and respect from whites since Reconstruction. I wonder how much one city can expect African-Americans to bear. Still, the Pearl alumni I spoke with are pleased that MLK is there, that their beloved school still resonates with student voices. "It's appropriate that it's a magnet school," Ms. Wynn told me, "because that continues the tradition of academic excellence in that building."

---

  In Nashville recently for a conference, with some time before church on Sunday morning, I decided to drive my old route to junior high, camera and notepad on the seat beside me, a CD of the Fisk Jubilee Singers in the stereo. Crossing Church Street, the school was visible in the distance. It hadn't been when I was in junior high. I realized, as I approached Charlotte Avenue, that the John Henry Hale Homes were gone. All of them, nearly 500 units, razed. According to a sign at the site, a federal grant called Hope VI would fund the construction of mixed-income, single-family townhouses in their place. I was troubled, at first, that so many units of affordable housing had been eliminated, but then I noticed just how small, how close together the concrete slab footprints of the old duplexes were. I wondered what had happened to the children whose homes once rested on those foundations—the children I'd swept past every morning on my way to school. They'd be in their twenties now.

  I climbed out of my car at King, feeling a stab of nostalgia despite myself. The building has been fixed up, with new concrete steps, shiny railings, and white metal window frames. Inside, the hallways we called "puke yellow" have been painted white and royal blue. Oddly, I missed the foreboding feel the school had commanded when I was young. Without the housing projects blocking the view, I could see the Nashville skyline and Tennessee State Capitol from the front steps. People were walking around the neighborhood, pushing strollers or just wandering. No one paid much attention to the white woman in the navy pea coat on the steps of Pearl High.

  I drove across the railroad tracks and walked around Fisk. It was the first time I'd ever been on any part of the campus beyond the athletic field. At a bus stop across the street, an elderly woman waited. She was dressed impeccably in a red wool dress suit with a matching wide-brimmed red hat, and she did not shy from the February wind. I wondered how many people at my church would show up if their only transportation was the city bus. I thought about offering this woman a ride to wherever she was going, but didn't, worried about offending her pride. The MTA bus pulled up and hydraulics hissed as the driver lowered the bus to sidewalk level. The woman shuffled aboard, the door closed, and they were gone. I walked around campus a little longer, taking pictures, and chastised myself when I saw that a campus clock read 10:25. My church, all the way out in Green Hills, began at 10:30. I was a long way from Green Hills, and would be very late.

I dashed over to my car and began the drive back to my part of town, counting down the familiar landmarks—first MLK, then the Krispy Kreme, Baptist Hospital, Vanderbilt University, the Pancake Pantry, the I-440 overpass, another mile down Hillsboro and I was there, climbing the steps at Calvary United Methodist. The minister was just ending the morning announcements. It was 10:35 and I had not been speeding. For the rest of the church service, I thought about the woman in the red wool dress, how distant she had seemed when actually, she was not so far away.

# LEAVE THE DRIVING TO US

P.U.M.P.K.I.N.

The secret societies finally piqued my interest. Our tour guide, a young woman wearing pleated khakis and a navy and orange windbreaker, had led us from the student center, past the quadrangle, and into a narrow stone courtyard. Today, I remember very little about the campus, and nothing specific about the members of my tour group beyond the guide's clothes and the palpable combination of boredom and anxiety pervading our little cluster of teenagers and their parents. The day had begun with rain showers and the courtyard smelled of new leaves and freshly turned soil. Though so much has faded, I remember clearly that, until the guide took us into that fragrant, mysterious garden, I'd been pretty certain that UVA was not the school for me.

The feeling of not belonging had come on fast. I'd taken the bus from Huntington, West Virginia that morning and while it trundled through the thick black of pre-dawn, I'd gazed into the lit windows in the subdivisions along Interstate 64, imagined families inside preparing for work and school on that April morning, and reflected, all dreamy and hazy, on where I would find my next home. I was a junior in high school. College, for years only an idea based on the well-thumbed copy of *The REAL Guide to College and Universities* beside my bed, was solidifying into an actual choice, one I'd have to make by the end of that year. As the bus continued east, I listened to a bootleg tape of They Might Be Giants performing live at Mountain Stage. The eerily appropriate lyrics pealed through my headphones: "At the end of the tour, when the road disappears, if there's any more people around when the tour runs aground, then meet at the end of the tour." I listened, felt the bus rumble, and thought about the University of Virginia. My college book told me to expect a studious, self-motivated student body, a strong sense of tradition, a good journalism program and lots of student-led clubs. On paper, it seemed wonderful. In the world of actual people, of flesh, mortar, and stone, I hadn't been on campus an hour before I wanted to catch the bus to William and Mary.

After all my careful considerations and planning, my hopes for UVA were derailed by clothing. *Clothing.* Never a fashion maven, I've always joked that lack of style *is* my style. At that point in my life, my friends either dressed like me or didn't care. For most of high school, I'd donned my father's old khakis, one of a selection of rock t-shirts, and my prized pair of cherry red Doc Marten's. This being the height of the 1990s thrift store/grunge trend, I fit right in with the crowd at my school.

But as our tour group circled campus that day, I felt self-conscious, even in the flowered periwinkle skirt and sleeveless blouse with faux tortoiseshell buttons meticulously selected from the racks at T.J. Maxx. UVA students seemed more dressed up for a typical Tuesday class than I was for the tour. The guide talked and I searched vainly for any glimpse of a plaid shirt or clunky shoes. No luck. "J. Crew U," one of my friends called it. "That's, like, some fancy catalogue, right?" I'd said back, utterly clueless. I'd heard of J. Crew and The Limited, but until I'd begun to see the world through a broader, college-bound lens, had no concept of their clothing being of noticeably superior quality to items from Stein Mart and T.J.; they were all dress clothes to me.

Unable to find anyone who matched my style, I prepared to endure my brief time on campus. I was staying in a dorm with the daughter of some family friends; she was going to take me to dinner that evening. Then we would attend a Fellowship of Christian Athletes meeting and hang out in the dorm. The next morning, I'd sit in on a journalism class and Habitat for Humanity meeting. I would be on a Greyhound bound for Norfolk before lunch, and I began counting the hours.

All that self-conscious squirming came before I stood in the close stone courtyard and saw a Z painted on the ground. Our guide told us about Z, IMP, P.U.M.P.K.I.N., and 7—UVA's most famous secret societies. Many of the societies devoted themselves to public service; some members never revealed their allegiances until their obituaries were printed. While the guide talked, I stopped looking for old Army jackets and entered a reverie. A band of eccentric Robin Hood types dodged through campus shadows while autumn leaves skittered about lampposts. I imagined my friends emerging from the shadows, perhaps in cloaks, all of us grinning silently, striding down the Lawn toward some good deed across campus. The secret societies appealed to everything I was looking for—tradition and quirk. I could belong to a group that was closed and self-defining while still reaching out into the larger community. Insular expansion.

### THE #2 BUS

I have said this before: When I think of my youth in Nashville, I think of being almost constantly in motion. At the time, it was almost oceanic, both relentless and invisible. Looking back, I realize how much of my life unfolded in conversations inside cars and city buses rolling between yellow and white lines, but my motion wasn't only vehicular. Sitting in class, I jiggled a knee and looked out the window. Even as a young child, hanging out with friends tended to involve some degree of roaming.

I grew up in the vast swath of the city with no sidewalks, only acre after acre lot, rancher after rancher, ridge after ridge rolling toward the horizon. In elementary and middle school, the lack of sidewalks drove us to wandering more than if we'd had point-to-point destinations lined out in concrete. First on foot and then on bicycle, my friends and I cut through yards and over cul de sacs. We waded Otter Creek and learned the layout of back yards on streets named after Confederate heroes. We stomped up gulleys—secret, rocky tunnels with honeysuckle roofs—and knew who had the most rosebushes; who'd tossed an old car battery; who had a playhouse, relic of children long since grown up and moved away, rotting in their backyard. We wandered, ambled, chewed on Airheads from the corner store, and talked, nearly always, about school and the events of the day.

Court-ordered busing meant that we moved to a new public school after fourth grade, again after sixth grade, and again after eighth grade. Thus, there was nearly always a looming decision—would you stay in your "zoned school," switch over to a private school, or try to get into a magnet school? Most of my friends from the neighborhood, swimming pool, and church were experts in pedagogical theory before we'd turned 10. When I was 11 and decided to attend a Magnet School my world broadened beyond that little corner of the city. My new friends and I sat in the back of a city bus, where the bench seats faced each other. We shared rumors about teachers and discussed the different parts of town we'd seen since making friends with kids from different neighborhoods. We gossiped about those kids, many of whom had thick Nashville accents and mullets or, worse, poof bangs. They lived in smaller houses and they occasionally revealed family truths like siblings in prison or grandparents getting trashed at family reunions, which were either completely foreign concepts or things we'd learned to cloak in whisper and euphemism. The kids from the other side of Nashville, though foreign on many levels, were also friendly and nerdy. I liked them, but did always feel some relief when I climbed on the #2 bus and headed out toward Belmont and Green Hills. These were my people.

As we became teenagers, our conversation topics shifted ever more often to our distant, unfathomable future. We all expected to go to college. In seventh grade, most of us at MLK, even the poof-bang and mullet kids from across town, took the S.A.T. as an exercise in determining our preparedness for the looming college search and a gauge of how smart we were. My scores earned me a degree of recognition and a slot in an ecology camp along the Georgia coast, wandering a wild beach with a cadre of aspiring marine biologists.

MLK didn't always feel like the school for me. In eighth grade the bus passed the Hume-Fogg Academic Magnet School every day and I couldn't get over how much *cooler* the kids seemed. Instead of mullets, I saw dreadlocks. They played Hackey Sack on the lawn and smoked clove cigarettes at the bus stop down the street. On the bus, they debated current events and spoke about college with a level of confidence and swagger the science kids at MLK didn't possess. Even the building, an imposing Gothic Revival with castle-esque turrets, seemed cooler. I transferred, without much hesitation, after ninth grade.

At Hume-Fogg, my college search amped up accordingly. I was 15 by then. My friends and I went to the college fair at the Green Hills Mall each September. Every Friday, the school hosted a "College Corner" in the hallway by the guidance office. Interested students could speak to an admissions representative from a college—sometimes state schools like Austin-Peay or MTSU, but often small private colleges like Kenyon, Williams, Bates, or Davidson. If a rep came from an Ivy League school, the line snaked down the hallway. At home, my family's dining room table was perpetually awash in the glossy, dream-like brochures put out by admissions departments.

I looked carefully at music and English programs and wanted to major in some type of writing, but my college search was absorbed not so much in the quest for education as the search for place. Would I study writing in Providence, Rhode Island, or New York City, or Sewanee, Tennessee? What was Oregon like? Would I enjoy the one-class-at-a-time schedule at Colorado College? At Hume-Fogg, nearly all of us were asking these questions. My education there was intense, challenging, and jubilant—fueled in equal parts by poetry, Jolt cola, and vague notions of old stone buildings in some distant town.

After getting our driver's licenses, my friends and I would often get coffee or ice cream, depending on the time of year, and drive aimlessly around Nashville. Inevitably, we wound up at Vanderbilt, wandering among deserted classroom buildings in the dark. We read flyers about student elections, parties, and paper-typing services, gazed into the lit windows of the Student Union, listened to the noise drifting over from Fraternity Row. Despite all those miles and miles we must have covered over countless weekends, we never entered a building. Content to troll the periphery of others' experiences, we knew we had to wait our turn.

I decided to visit schools over that spring break when I was 16. I couldn't afford airfare and didn't have my driver's license. When my great-uncle called and invited me to visit him in Newport News and tour William and Mary, I had a brainstorm: Hop a Greyhound from Nashville to Huntington, then on across the Virginias. In the process, visit Marshall University, the University of Virginia, and the College of William and Mary. I'd also pass through the college towns of Richmond and Blacksburg.

For a week in April, the Greyhound bus could take me on the search I'd dreamed of since seventh grade. I just had to climb on board.

**THE HONOR CODE**

After the tour at UVA was over, my host, Stephanie, met me on the Lawn. I really only knew her through a mutual friend at church, but our lives had enough similarities that it wasn't difficult to converse with her. Like me, she'd grown up in Green Hills and attended public schools. (Unlike me, she'd been quite popular and had a serious boyfriend for all four years of high school.) Our younger siblings were classmates, and our families both belonged to the Seven Hills Swim and Tennis Club. We both had musical fathers, though hers was the director of the Vanderbilt University band and mine merely a dabbler in clarinet and saxophone. Even so, Dr. Sagen invited my father and me to play with the Vandy pep band every Christmas, while the students were away.

Stephanie and I walked to the school bookstore, where I purchased two t-shirts: UVA Swimming for my sister and UVA Cycling for myself (UVA Athletics shirts were very "in" in our portion of Nashville at the time). When we walked to the dining hall for dinner, I left my purchases and backpack outside, thrilled to be bound, even temporarily, to the principles of the school's Honor Code.

"You mean no one steals anything?" I asked as I placed my bag in the long line of Jansports and L.L. Beans on the sidewalk. The sky was striking an orange hue over Jefferson's famed Rotunda. I wondered if I shouldn't carry my wallet, Walkman, and journal in with me, just in case.

"No one steals *anything*," said Stephanie. "The Honor Code is a huge tradition here. No one would mess it up because everyone has an equal share in it, you know?"

On UVA's campus that April, Stephanie exuded the casually confident air of someone who had found what I was still looking for. Like my tour guide, she wore a UVA windbreaker. The fact that I had known her in Nashville and followed her application and matriculation process from afar made her even more inspiring than my guide, and she was equally passionate about Mr. Jefferson's University. We ate dinner from trays at a long wooden table, Stephanie stopping every few minutes to greet a friend and introduce me. I tried as best I could to be complimentary about the school, mentioning that I was impressed by the array of student activities, including the secret societies. Stephanie was eager to talk up Virginia.

"You can do anything you want here, you just have to take the initiative to make it happen," she said.

Another pearl of wisdom: "You learn so much about yourself and other people in college. Really, I knew nothing in high school. When you're in high school, you just don't know anything." That comment stuck for the rest of my college search. What was behind the curtain? What did I not know?

After dinner and the FCA meeting, she studied in the library while I used email for the first time and wrote in my journal. We crossed campus in the cool dark and stayed up late, talking with her suitemates, finally getting around to a debate about whether or not UVA students were apathetic. Stephanie staunchly supported her school. After a time, her new not-quite boyfriend came over and they showed off the moves they'd learned in a ballroom dancing class. As the boy swung Stephanie into an elegant dip, the suitemates and I exchanged looks. *These two really have a thing for each other*, we said without speaking. Another little thrill of acceptance.

At about two a.m., I unrolled a sleeping bag and drifted off to sleep while Stephanie and her roommate talked about the boy. I'd been awake for nearly 24 hours and felt as though I'd moved through every type of place. I was content to let any thoughts of going to Marshall University, which I'd visited the day before I came to UVA, fade away. Marshall seemed too utilitarian. The kids there wanted a college education and weren't as enamored with the idea of a University Experience as the UVA students. There was no Honor Code. Their dorms were merely places to live, not organized into suites to foster a sense of community. They went home over the weekends or went to school part time and worked part time. They had to. I wanted the total experience, not just the degree at the end. I thought of what I'd experienced since I'd left Huntington—darkness, mountains, buses with sticky floors, libraries, misty evenings, boyfriends, conversations, and ideas. In my dreams that night, the floor rocked like a Greyhound.

The next morning, I tagged along to the Habitat for Humanity meeting and a journalism class. There was not an adult in sight at the meeting. Charlottesville proper was visible from the windows of the chapter house. The homes were bunched closely on a hillside. After the meeting, we walked back toward the center of campus, through one of the famous pavilions and another stone courtyard, over to class. This was more of the UVA I'd come to expect. The professor wore a bow tie and passed out an article and a political cartoon, both addressing NAFTA. The class sat around the table and debated the rhetorical merits of each argument. I loved it, and even spoke up, but felt nothing but squirming doubt as I looked around the room—were these people really like me at all?

### THE GREYHOUND

Although I appreciated Mr. Jefferson's university by the end of my visit, I still felt a surge of relief when I climbed back onto the Greyhound. Parameters were much clearer there. The bus was four seats plus an aisle wide and about 40 feet long. It traveled along a fixed path—sometimes the Interstate, but more often, two and four-lane highways.

There was also an accepted cultural protocol for the bus. Families or lovers gravitated toward the bench seats in the back; older riders sat up front. I always chose a window seat and never talked to anyone until I'd pulled out my journal and listened to a couple songs on my Walkman. Establishing my own agenda before talking provided an out if my seatmate proved tiresome, intoxicated, or excessively strange. Even so, on every leg of that trip, I'd had a conversation. I'd met a fighter pilot; a woman from Hawaii; a woman who had fled her husband and moved to California, but was returning East to be reunited with her children; a Cherokee man with a long, thick braid who claimed he'd never been sick in his life. After every trip, I'd come away feeling enlightened and amazed that the world, let alone one bus, could contain so many divergent stories. "Travelers together are all alone," I wrote in my journal.

---

I felt comfortable on the Greyhound, even though most of my traveling companions were even less like me than the UVA students I'd just left. We *were* together and alone all at once. Not only was our physical space definable, but we would only be with each other for a limited time. Beyond the "would I want that person sitting next to me" assessment, I didn't think much about what the other passengers were wearing or doing. Because we knew we would never see each other again, folks shared their life stories freely, confessed wrongdoings and regrets without hesitation. The Cherokee man and a pretty blonde even struck up a romance that lasted from Louisville to Lexington.

I already understood that class differences existed and that college was a vague, distant concept for many people. On the bus, my stories about campus tours, soccer, and Advanced Placement History might have been as foreign to my seatmates as theirs were to me, but, due to my own family history, I didn't feel as removed as I probably should have. Of my four grandparents, only my father's mother had a degree beyond high school, one she attained laboriously over 10 years of night school while raising three children. Her youngest son, my father, attended the University of Pennsylvania. My mother, only one generation removed from a sharecroppers' shack in Alabama on her mother's side, had a degree in economics from the University of Delaware. For me, their oldest child, college was never a question. I had Northwestern and Penn t-shirts, a Fighting Blue

Hens overnight bag. Even my mother's mother, whose formal education ended in the fourth grade, had purchased enough Alabama memorabilia to ensure that I never went day in my infancy without wearing something that was either red or had an elephant on it.

College was as much a part of my present and future as driving a car. However, I still, somehow, managed to see education after high school as a choice. Whenever cousins down in Alabama told me they'd be going to Fayette County Community College, I'd smile and nod while wondering why they hadn't set their sights any higher. When I toted my backpack full of AP Study Guides onto the Greyhound and engaged in conversation with a young man who had gone straight into the Navy after high school, I thought, "What an interesting choice. It sure takes all kinds." I thought I was gregarious and nonjudgmental, and I probably was, but I never really understood that everyone else didn't have the array of choices that I had.

### THE WREN PORTICO

The day which had begun in a sleeping bag on the floor of a dorm in Charlottesville, found me, at sunset, riding shotgun in my 81-year-old great-uncle's Geo Metro. As we always did when I visited him, we were driving from his house in Newport News to look at the warships docked in Norfolk. Along with t-shirts and fashionably torn pants, my identity in high school was very much tied up in being a peacenik, but I had no qualms gawking at the destroyers and aircraft carriers. Uncle David was family, a war veteran, the brother of the grandfather who had died before I was born. We'd been going down to the docks since I was a young child. The ships were stunning and the Navy boys, I noticed, for the first time, were not much older than me and kind of cute.

This was the first time I'd visited Uncle David without my parents. With my mom, his niece, conversation inevitably turned to relatives I had never met. When it was just me, I could talk about anything I wanted. We ate dinner at a Shoney's and I asked Uncle David about his teaching career—he'd taught chemistry at a private school for 20 years. Sitting in Norfolk with miles of thinking behind me, I'd decided that it might be fun to be an English teacher. I told Uncle David I'd like to be a teacher, a minister, or some sort of writer. Over watery coffee and a piece of hot fudge cake, we discussed the merits of each profession. Uncle David told me about his career, which I soon realized was not only family history, but also a narrative account of the American history I'd been boning up on for my upcoming exam.

Uncle David told me that his family ate hot dogs for dinner every Saturday night, a tradition which began out of necessity during the Great Depression, but continued on down the line to my own family's weekend meals. Uncle David enlisted in the Army years before Pearl Harbor and remained, working as a chemist, until the early 1960s. He started teaching practically on a whim and retired from the same school after two decades. These stories, more than the Greyhound's, were mine.

The next morning, I rose early and inspected the living room. The carpet was green shag and sweet whiffs of pipe tobacco seemed to escape the fibers with each step I took. There was the picture my mother had taken of Uncle David and Aunt Lileth, who had been dead for 10 years. I flipped through the yearbooks of the high school where he'd taught and inspected a framed photograph of him and my grandfather, standing in their uniforms shortly after the liberation of Paris. My uncle seemed much the same, just younger. The grandfather I'd never met looked at the camera as if he alone knew the punch line to a joke. His airman's cap sat askew on his head. His edges in the photograph were just a little blurry. Like me, he seemed to be someone who enjoyed motion, who remained still only long enough for the camera to capture him.

---

I remember even less about William and Mary that I do about UVA. I imagine this is because I had already heard the speech about tough admissions standards but SATs not meaning everything, had become so adept at touring and analyzing and moving through spaces, that I was able to skim through my experience at William and Mary and glean my realities off the top. When I was on campus, looking at the Christopher Wren building and feeling the warmth of a sunny day, I felt like I could belong there, too. Our guide told us about traditions at the College. Every new student, she said, walks through the portico in the Wren Building and is greeted by all the other students and faculty on the other side. Four years later, the walk is reversed and they walk through the portico for Commencement in the building's courtyard. Every Christmas, the school hosted a giant Yule Log Party with storytellers and punch. UVA might be known as Mr. Jefferson's University, but William and Mary was his actual college—the school he had attended. It sounded like a thoughtful, enchanting place to be.

But it didn't fit. I don't know why. Maybe it was the flatness of the Tidewater region. Maybe I felt odd about attending school next to Williamsburg—an off-putting colonial theme park. Most likely, though, it was that the coast of Virginia was just a little too far from Nashville. I liked W&M enough to apply there, but it simply didn't hold the same allure as UVA.

The University of Virginia wasn't me, but maybe it could be. I could go there and be in a secret society and live in a room on the Lawn and become an expert in journalism and American history. I could work for the *Cavalier Daily* and stay up late and have interesting discussions around a seminar table about politics with a professor wearing a bow tie. And what's wrong with J. Crew anyway? When I had to look nice, I already went prep anyway. I could work a job over the summer and save up money, convert my wardrobe. I was in love with the idea of UVA and what it represented—the very University-ness of it. I formally visited about half a dozen more colleges before I applied to the one where I'd end up. In every tour, I asked if they had an Honor Code or, if not that, a crew team.

However, if those schools were where I saw myself going in just over a year, the Greyhound was where I was at the moment—the anchoring experience of the entire tour. I wanted, from college, the same casual confidence of belonging I felt when I hit <PLAY> on my Walkman and the world unrolled past my window. I also wanted the thrill of going somewhere, of rounding a curve and seeing a town tucked in a valley. I wanted to learn, as I did on the bus, about new lives and stories. I wanted to write them all down. I believed, falsely and romantically, that life would not be nearly as complicated in college as it had been in high school. Once I settled in, I would have a life like Stephanie's, or perhaps any number of Pulitzer winners who had come before me. Meals in the dining hall, club meetings, studying in the library, classes around seminar tables, dancing lessons with a boyfriend, political discussions in the dorms. Insular expansion, a cocooned life, all the while growing and learning. If only I could find that school—and maybe it was UVA. I believed in the myth of the image.

Greyhound created images, too, of course. We stopped frequently in little stations and major hubs. In each one, part of their ad campaign was different reasons to take the bus. Poster after poster depicted kids arriving safely at grandma's, old friends reunited, children coming home from an extended absence—like the Army or college. I'd never considered taking Greyhound before, but those ads made me feel like I was a part of something vast and exciting. I'd discovered some elemental piece of Americana. While nearly everyone I'd encountered on the buses was indeed heading toward or away from someone they loved, they usually didn't match the brochure. People traveled for days to attend funerals or be reunited with estranged children or flee abusive husbands. Nary a weekend visit to grandma among them.

## THE COZY HOME DINER

The last day of my trip was Good Friday. I planned to get on the bus in Norfolk, ride for nearly 20 hours back to Nashville, sleep all day Saturday, and sing with the church choir Easter morning. Uncle David woke me up at five a.m. so I could catch the 6:50 bus.

If I'd had my way, we would have stopped at a McDonald's somewhere between Newport News and Norfolk and gotten a sausage biscuit and a Coke—not a typical breakfast for me, but something my family called road food. Uncle David, generations removed from my way of seeing, zipped the Geo past one fast food joint after another. When we arrived in downtown Norfolk at six, plenty of time before my bus was supposed to roll out, we put my stuff in a locker at the station and walked back out into the street.

"We'll eat there," he said, pointing across the street to a diner with a sign above the door which said, in big yellow letters, "The Cozy Home," and had a picture of a plate and a fork.

Honestly, I hadn't even noticed the place; I'd been scanning the street for fast food or a donut shop. But when I saw it, I knew it was the perfect way to close out my trip. I had traveled through Kentucky, across West Virginia and Virginia, and felt as though I'd tapped into the heart of the country. I had spoken to seatmates living vastly different lives from my own, had seen the sun rise and set from the Appalachians to the Tidewater. I'd visited universities named for Chief Justice John Marshall and the King and Queen of England, with one designed by Thomas Jefferson in the middle. I'd heard a lot about ideals and traditions at each school, believed in them, felt myself striving toward my own place where collective ideals could become my own. With all this tradition, all this vast experience, and all this future coming to a point on a Greyhound bus trip, why not wrap it all up at an old-fashioned diner?

The Cozy Home smelled of grease and biscuits and cigarettes. Its walls were yellow with brown trim. Its clientele was entirely African-American, and they spoke in the low murmur of regulars. The waitress and cook were also black. I could see the cook in the back, flipping hash browns, loading plates, ringing a bell when another order was up. The waitress walked past me, grabbed the plate without speaking, turned, and set it in front of a man wearing a trucker cap. He unrolled his fork and went to work on some biscuits and gravy.

At every other point on the trip, my memory of race is almost non-existent. I just didn't notice it, and I don't mean that I was "post-racial" or color blind. I mean that I almost certainly didn't notice people who weren't white because I wasn't looking for them. I do remember that on the bus, African-Americans seemed much more likely than whites to be traveling in large family units. As a result, I rarely sat by them. I'm also certain that when I scanned seats and looked for people to sit with who looked "safe" or "like me," I would have chosen a young white person. On the campuses, as I analyzed the dress and demeanor of each collective student body, I would, once again, have been looking for people like me I could be friends with.

I remember that everyone else in the diner was black because that mattered, for just a split second, after I opened the door and proceeded to the counter. Then I caught myself, mid-wince, shoved the prejudices to the bottom of my thought pile, and sat down, pleased with myself once again, ready to enjoy the authenticity of the Cozy Home Diner.

The waitress who had served up the biscuits and gravy was on the phone—a heavy plastic one, bolted to the wall next to where my uncle and I took our seats. I figured we would have to wait a minute or two for her to get off the phone. I caught bits of her conversation as I took in the atmosphere at the counter.

"She was supposed to come in at 5:45," the woman said, twirling the cord around her fingers. The bell rang, she turned again and slid the hash browns under a man who was reading the *USA Today*.

The clock on the wall was big and round, lit dull yellow from the back, and ringed with pink neon. The hands had turned to the six and two. I realized this woman had probably been working all night, and sat up eagerly—*what stories she must have!*

"I'm not filling in for her," the woman said. She picked up an empty plate and slid it back through the window. The customer left his money on the counter. The door had a brass bell that rang when he left.

"We won't be served here," Uncle David said.

"She's on the phone," I said. "She hasn't seen us yet."

"You have to come in. I'm not staying," the waitress said. Two men across the counter from us started to talk about the newspaper.

The hands on the clock were on the six and three when the waitress said, "Okay," and rubbed her face as though she was very tired. I knew she'd see us when she returned the phone to its cradle, which was right next to my uncle's head. But when she hung up the phone, she turned her head completely away from us and set the phone down without looking. She turned her back and spoke to the men with the paper. Obviously, they all knew the woman who had apparently decided to skip work. The waitress took their plates and, once again, managed to turn and slide them through the window to the kitchen without looking at us.

"Come on, Erin." My uncle knew. I had an idea, only the vaguest one, that we were being ignored. But surely not, I kept thinking. Surely not.

"Just a moment longer," I said. The waitress continued talking with the two men, her back turned to us. She turned to another man, wrote his order down on a pad. The bell rang. She took a plate from the window, ripped the paper from her pad and handed it to the cook, turned with the plate. Steam rose up from the eggs and my stomach growled. The waitress set it down in front of a man just two seats away. Her uniform was yellow and brown, like the décor. The man sitting closest to us raised his hand and asked for the check. The waitress took his plate, her arm almost brushing my own, but neither of them looked at me. She turned her back again and I stared at it, dumbstruck. Her apron was tied in the back with a bow, like I'd seen in old movies. The tie had grease stains on it. My uncle sat beside me, his hands folded in front of him. He slid the menu back between the sugar and the napkin holder. I leaned forward. "Excuse me," I said. She didn't move. I stared at her back for a little longer. The hands on the clock had almost joined at six. Just a little longer, I thought.

"You'll miss your bus," said my uncle.

"You're right. Let's go."

At first, I learned the obvious lesson in the diner where I couldn't get breakfast. It was a taste, however small, of what it's like to be refused something you want because of the color of your skin. When we left the diner, that's the first thing my uncle said to me—that I was fortunate, that I should never forget what just happened, that whites so rarely have the opportunity to experience any degree of rejection based on skin color.

Though I didn't realize it until later, the Cozy Home Diner also revealed that a great deal of my trip was a sham. I had bounced, blithely and eagerly, between a world full of choices and a world full of limitations. My bus mates, the men and women in the café, the tired faces in the stations and towns along the way—most of them couldn't decide whether or not they'd like to wear J. Crew and go to a school with a crew team or Honor Code, because that was not an option for them. I had reveled in the simplicity of bus travel, never considering that what I saw as simple was, for others, either a dead end or an immensely complex web to navigate.

Later I decided that this woman took from me my ability to learn her story, and she mine. I will never know what she experienced at the hands of whites to make her act the way she did. She'll never know who I was. Maybe she'd heard enough awkward apologies. Maybe, as well-meaning as I was, I would have said something offensive or ignorant and she, a woman who was old enough to have been turned away from lunch counters herself, had just had enough. Her replacement wasn't coming in, and she wasn't going to serve us. Or maybe my uncle and I had walked into a secret society that we were unaware of. We'll never know. We'll never know because no pleasantries were traded, no stories revealed, no reasons given. We sat at the counter; no one looked at us; my uncle allowed me to stay there until it sank in. We left. I had plenty of money, so after I'd hugged Uncle David goodbye, I headed to the vending machines. I ate Dunkin Stix, drank orange juice from a plastic cup with a foil top, and listened to the Indigo Girls wail about Nashville through my headphones. "As I drive from your pearly gates, I realize that I just can't stay. All those mountains, they kept you locked inside, hid the truth from my slighted eyes." The bus rolled out of Norfolk and back across the Chesapeake Bay.

## BACK HOME

I returned to Nashville at two a.m. wearing the same outfit I'd left in—a vintage Phys. Ed. hoodie from my high school, Levis, Tevas. "Do I look older, Mom?" I asked. I felt older, leaner, more certain of uncertainty, which was something I probably couldn't have tolerated before the trip. "Not really," she said.

Since we were so rarely up at two a.m., we deviated from the normal route home and went to the Krispy Kreme on Thompson Lane. I knew

Thompson Lane well enough, but appreciated the strangeness of the landscape in the middle of the night.

"You got a ton of college brochures while you were gone," Mom said.

"Ugh," I said.

"I don't want them on the dining room table any more. Take them up to your room and sort through them. I know they could use some at Stratford. They don't have any."

I thought this was a great idea. Stratford was a poor, mostly black school across the Cumberland River. A family friend was a guidance counselor there. It pleased me to know that some kid might pick up a brochure to Eckerd College and decide to major in marine biology there. All I had to do was sort through and decide on all the schools I definitely didn't want to go to.

I slept past noon the next day; then, as ordered, slid from my bed to the floor and sorted through college brochures. Full of the experience of thinking about college—tired, even, of the opportunities—I decided to throw away any brochure without a picture that immediately grabbed me. One college I'd never heard of, Carnegie Mellon, had a shot on the inside of a cyclist going past a stone building in early morning mist. That building is where I lived, two years later, as a freshman.

My mom came in to see how it was going.

"That's a big pile," she said. "You've really narrowed it down."

"Yeah."

"Well, this will make the guidance department at Stratford pretty happy. Bring the box down when you're done."

I didn't want to go to a school that didn't have a crew team. This didn't mean I would row; frankly, I wasn't sure of that either. But even though I understood, by the end of the trip, that life is not a lark through college brochure-esque universes, I couldn't shake their appeal—the notion that it was something I could be, that life at school would be filled with fall foliage, close friends, and clear purpose. Later, minoring in design, I would study the effects of images—how advertisers don't dupe so much as consumers play into the illusion. We cannot contain our desire for something better, for a pleasant space, for something that will make us fit. "Picture Yourself Here," said the CMU brochures. "Leave the Driving to Us," said the Greyhound posters. In a sense, that desire drowned out the sound of my sneakers on a concrete path, the tour guides, the trepidation, the tiredness. But for a moment in a diner in Norfolk, nothing spoke louder than that back turned to me, the averted eyes, the voice in my head that demanded, "Look at me!" For a moment, it was what I could not even desire or ask for that I wanted.

Then I went home, sat on my floor, spread out the brochures, and plucked up my future like a daffodil on a cold spring day.

# ROWING THROUGH THE RUINS

### THE WARM-UP

E very day began in darkness that spring when I learned about sight. Perhaps that is why I saw so well.

---

Sight is more than eyes. Sight is the morning, one of many, that I ran through Bloomfield in the dark, the rhythm of feet on asphalt. I ran past darkened houses, their windows empty stares. Sight is wondering who has lived in those houses. There was an Italian bakery at the top of East Liberty Street. The stronger the smell of baking bread, the closer we were to the end of our climb. I heard the quickening pace of 10 pairs of sneakers, and we crested the hill in groups of twos and threes, illuminated mid-stride by the yellow rectangle of light from the bakery door. Looking inside as I ran past, I saw two men, one with a mustache, holding a ball of dough that was beginning to ooze past his fingertips, staring out at us. It was 5:30 in the morning.

The first glimpse of the river came and went quickly. That early in the morning, the Allegheny was merely a yawning absence of light with the 31st Street Bridge arching across it. In the instant before more rowhouses and a peeling billboard blocked my view, I could see the current rippling in the reflections of streetlights on the water. The pre-dawn air was infused with spring and the spindly landscaping trees we passed were beginning to bud. I felt the energy stirring beneath the bark and ran faster. Liberty Street curved into the remains of an industrial district along the river. We plunged toward the void.

———•—•—•———

That spring, my junior year at Carnegie Mellon, was the last spring of the 20th century. I took Reading the Built Landscape from Dave Demarest, a professor with gray muttonchops and perfectly round wire-rimmed glasses. I'd already taken classes in photography and design and fallen in love with form—the line a red-tile roof makes against a blue sky, the repetition of shapes in a row of houses, the perfect weight and curve of a Coca-Cola bottle, transient webs of light and shadow. I thought Demarest's class would be more of the same, but he focused instead on the functions of cityscapes. He told us that we could analyze them as thoroughly as any book. We learned that suburbs, interstates, prisons, and public parks often reveal the collective values of the society that created them.

Demarest's expertise centered on the neighborhoods and industrial ruins of Pittsburgh and that is what he loved to teach. We sat around a seminar table during his lectures, and my quads ached from my morning row through the city. I had rowed every fall and spring since my freshman year and thought I had seen Pittsburgh. Not so, Demarest said; you have never really seen this place until you learn that Pittsburgh has grown from its rivers and the work they have supported. Then you will realize that it is all layers, that some of the layers peek through the others, like sheets beneath a frayed blanket.

———•—•—•———

The Three Rivers Rowing Club is on Herr's Island, its boathouse tucked in the corner of an office park, facing a narrow channel and the towering face of Troy Hill. Several teams row from it, including Carnegie Mellon's. A hundred years before I joined the team, the island's docks teemed with livestock being driven to the slaughterhouse. Factory sounds rang out over the squeals of pigs; the air was thick and smoky; the combined smells of industry and death were heavy, inescapable. One entire end of the island, which now supports an upscale housing development, was covered in entrails and hides.

But I belonged to another generation drawn to work along, and within, the current. What I remember are the fluorescent lights spilling from the team bays, rowers in Tevas and spandex carrying oars and boats. For *our* early mornings, the air was filled with commands from the coxswains: "Everyone, hands on the four! Ready for up to shoulders—and up! Watch the riggers!" We were students, but we owed two hours every morning to the river, our boat mates, and the quest for the perfect row—when all the rowers in a boat move as one body and carry the boat forward; when the boat itself balances on the center of its keel and responds to the power from the oars.

In rowing parlance, a balanced boat is "set" and forward momentum is "run." Rowers can make an unbalanced boat move quickly, but it won't have run. Instead, it will slow down, or check, slightly, as each oar is dropped in the water; and the rowers, the engine of the boat, will burn themselves out. Rowing is the art of efficient power. As we pushed off the dock and began our warm-up, I felt tense and focused. A train rumbled by across the channel and breathed like an animal over our shoulders.

---

Early in the semester, Demarest showed us a painting of the young George Washington, a surveyor, standing on a hill and pointing down at the confluence of two rivers. We recognized it immediately as Pittsburgh before the bridges and Three Rivers Stadium, those hillsides nothing but undulating forest. A line from Washington's journal served as the caption: "I spent some time in viewing the rivers, and the land in the fork; which I think is extremely well-suited for a fort as it has absolute command of both rivers." Before he climbed that mountain in December, 1753, 21-year-old Washington had crossed the ice-choked Allegheny in a flatboat. He fell in and almost drowned near the site of what is now the 40th Street Bridge.

---

We rowed out of the channel clumsily, not yet in sync, our muscles not fully awakened. We always waited slightly upstream from the 40th Street Bridge for the rest of the team. Our boat drifted with the current, so we took strokes occasionally to avoid the stone pilings. The size of the Allegheny took me aback every time we entered it.

From the water, the bridge itself seemed as high as any skyscraper and the occasional truck rolling over its joints sent echoes off the footers around us. In 1923, the newly completed triple-arched structure was named Washington's Crossing Bridge. I don't know how Washington did it. Even with the city all around, the view from the water made me feel vulnerable and insignificant. Trees rose up from the shoreline, causing the land to appear high and distant. Above them, orderly rows of lights marched down to the river. Without sunlight, the water seemed black and bottomless.

Except for the coxswain, who steered, we all faced backwards. I rowed in the bow seat of a four-person boat. We taped a flashlight to the decking behind me every morning to alert barges to our presence. The yellow sputtering bulb only broadened my understanding of the darkness. Barges displace water by the ton, yet are amazingly stealthy. Almost every crew has a near-miss story. As a barge passed silently in the middle of the river, our boat rolled and bounced pitifully in its wake. I thought about Washington, about the history that would not have been written had he drowned in that spot.

## ROWING UPSTREAM

I've learned that cities are built on the ruins of cities that were themselves built on the ruins of cities. What builds cities, or anything, but work and dreams? The fort envisioned by Washington defended British territories from the French and later played a role in the American Revolution. The rivers that made such an ideal location for a military post also situated Pittsburgh at the forefront of western commerce and industry. When the fort was dismantled in 1792, its pieces were used to build houses in the growing city. We often rowed past the fountain and state park that mark the site where Fort Pitt once stood and the Ohio River begins.

As the 19th century dawned, grist mills, printing shops, glass makers, and iron works thrived in the city. Coal was mined from the very hills Washington had walked. Pittsburgh's rivers surged and frothed with barges, cargo ships, and paddlewheelers. James Parton, a journalist passing through Pittsburgh in 1868, gave the city a lasting name and reputation: "If anyone would enjoy a spectacle as striking as Niagara," he wrote, "he may do so simply by walking up a long hill to Cliff Street in Pittsburg and looking over into—hell with the lid taken off."

Even then, the city's potential for work was largely untapped. Seven years later, in 1875, Andrew Carnegie, having noted the problems with maintaining iron train tracks and the expense of importing steel rails from England, brought the first high-volume steel mill to Pittsburgh. More followed. By the 1940s, Pittsburgh was producing more steel than the entire Soviet Union. There was so much smoke that streetlights were left on 24 hours a day. Then, through the 1970s and '80s, as American demand for steel dwindled and it became cheaper to import it, most of the mills closed. When I rowed in the 1990s, I looked up, not down, at what Parton would consider hell's smoldering remains—its glowing orange coals. Iron pipes protruded from the shore, stone staircases and abandoned railroad bridges led to nothing, factory roofs jutted over the trees; all of it an endless repetition of shape and form, all of it silent and watching. The summer after I took Reading the Built Landscape, the last brick smokestacks in the city limits were torn down—six towers along the Monongahela.

Rowing upstream beneath those crumbling remains of Carnegie's vision, we felt the weight of our own hopes in the dark. Beneath our striving muscles, our collective struggle for balance, our minds hummed with the stories we hoped to tell one day. Off river, we were college students carrying our separate dreams. In the current, we thought only of blending power and technique. We understood and read the noise made by fiberglass seats moving up the metal slide, an oar catching in the water, the swirl of the river as we pulled the oar through. For all of us, a balanced and moving boat meant the universe had clicked into place, but it was difficult to maintain. As soon as someone shifted her weight, pushed her oar out of the water too soon, or succumbed to the desire to take a light stroke, the boat would flop to one side and send oars chattering along the surface. The flawless rower would be an engine. She would never lean too far back at the finish or rush up the slide. She wouldn't pause at the catch; she would push through the drive with violent and beautiful force. And she would never, ever doubt herself. We hugged the south shore of the river and I wondered, "How long can I row solidly, without mistakes?" Passing silently beneath low-slung mill buildings, I thought only finish, arms away, slide, catch, drive. Match the other oars, match their hand heights and the angle of their backs, a thousand times in a row. It was still dark. The factories were hollow sentries above us.

More than 70,000 men were employed in the mills at the turn of the 20th century, most of them immigrants recruited from the farmlands of Europe. The nature of the work they did in the mills veered sharply from the work and dreams of their fathers. Millworkers were not skilled craftsmen or agrarians—they were the fuel of the fire and smoke of the Industrial Revolution, pieces of a vast machine. While their wives and children settled on the hillsides around the city, the men walked down to the river every morning and worked 12-hour shifts with only one day off every two weeks. They loaded and unloaded furnaces, stoked fires, stood watch as liquid flame was cast into ingots, and repeated this endlessly. I have seen pictures of them presiding over rivers of molten metal, with grease-blackened faces and biceps bulging under thin work shirts. They went weeks without seeing sunlight.

---

I liked to tell my non-rowing friends that when I woke up in the morning, dawn wasn't even a promise. Noah and his crew had a better understanding of land beyond the flood than I had of sunlight when practice began. But when we turned our boats downstream, the thinnest of olive branches appeared in the sky: a yellow and pink ribbon stretched over the contours of Polish Hill. It grew steadily wider as I watched the night sky diminishing. The pale blue dawn with the yellow and pink bands looked like an Easter Egg. Like hope.

---

Demarest loved industrial ruins. In class, he showed us slides featuring pictures of himself standing on piles of rubble, peering into the spherical structure of a brick furnace, leaning against smokestacks, his round glasses fitted with dark lenses against the sunlight. "These are our Roman Baths," he told us as he flashed a slide of a rusted blast furnace—"Our Parthenon, our Coliseum. When archeologists dig up the American 20th century, this is what they will find. What does that say about us?" It says that workers who rarely saw the sun, who wore grease and soot like permanent bruises, laid the foundation for our own layer of life. They founded the neighborhoods—the Italians in Bloomfield, the Poles—Polish Hill, the Germans—Troy Hill.

We saw all these neighborhoods from the river, heard them waking up, noticed the falling down and empty houses. But until that spring, I had never noticed the work or its remains, the accomplishments of men who lived on the hillsides, who walked to the buildings we saw from the water, and laid the framework for our cities. In the English Department's main office, rusted wheels and cogs and pitted chunks of coal that Demarest had collected were displayed under glass, like museum pieces

---

Some teams rowed downtown, under the glimmering skyscrapers, past the park commemorating Washington's fort, and onto the Ohio River, every morning. We always rowed far upstream first, then turned our boats and did a series of workouts—called "pieces"—into downtown. Because the water was calmer there, we spent most of our practice upstream, beneath the remains of Pittsburgh's industrial district. We marked how long we had been rowing by the landmarks we passed.

Usually, we could only see pieces of things. There were paddle-wheelers turned houseboats, then the fence surrounding the go-kart track, the top of a rusted crane, refueling docks for barges, a row of tunnels, the high corrugated metal wall of a factory with windows broken by vandals, a long stretch of wooden docks and crooked pilings. I used to prefer rowing downtown, where the river was bordered by a clean new walking path and glass-fronted buildings, but that spring I learned to keep my eyes soft as we rowed upstream. I could see the other rowers' shoulders, sense if we were moving in unison, and also see the river beyond them. A partially sunken barge met its own reflection; vines wound through the wheels of a train on an abandoned spur; a row of yellow-brick coke ovens, which resembled beehives, guarded the shoreline.

The sunrise revealed water like glass. With the dawn came the sounds of a city waking itself: compression brakes on the bridge above us, construction equipment and train whistles in the distance. Work long completed and work not yet begun converged at the water. Beneath the ruins, we cast about for form and function as if its residue still hung in the air. I believe it did. I know that men built and ran the machines now rusting around us. I could peel back the layers of time, rediscover the work and the dreams.

### DOWNTOWN SPEED WORK

In the middle of practice, Coach Oliver let us rest and stretch. Then he motored the coach's launch a little closer and brought a megaphone to his mouth. "Four minutes on. Two minutes off. Down to the Point. Racing starts." Four minutes—about 1,000 meters. It's probably 7,000 meters from here to the Point, Washington's triangle where the Ohio River begins.

"Staggered starts, women's four, you're first."

We moved our seats three-quarters of the way up the slide and dropped our oars in. I centered the balls of my feet, prepared to apply all my weight to them. Then, I shifted nervously, made sure my back was straight and matched the angle of the back in front of me, took deep breaths to enjoy the oxygen while I still could. Our coxswain's voice crackled through the small speaker attached to the hull. "Ladies? Racing start into a power 10. Then 10 to settle. Are you ready?" Silence, oxygen, the highway rumbling overhead. "ROW!"

The water swirled and frothed around our blades. We knew to shorten our strokes to get the boat moving. Our coxswain, Laura, called out the lengths of our slides. "Three-quarters!" We jumped off our feet, popped the oar out and returned halfway up the slide, caught as she yelled, "Half!" Then, "Three-quarters!" "Building!" "Full!" "Power 10, ladies!" Laura counted 10 strokes. The boat rocked, but we were moving fast. We hit 38 strokes per minute during the power 10 and needed to stay at a 30 for the rest of the piece.

It took a little less than a minute to start the boat, complete a power ten, and settle into 30 strokes per minute. For another 30 seconds, our adrenaline carried us. Then we noticed our ragged breaths, our burning quads. I realized I was slouching as if curving my chest would somehow bring in more air. Fatigue undermined my good intentions.

When I straightened my back, the boat rocked to one side. "None of that, ladies!" Laura yelled. On the North shore, a coal train whistled and in my oxygen-deprived state, it sounded like the whistle was both above and within me. "You hear that train?" Laura said. "You *are* that train! Don't you dare let anyone else carry your weight! We're doing a power 10 when that train reaches us! Take it up in two …one….two!" The counting was drowned out by the shriek of steel on steel, the thunder of the cars flying past. I gasped for breath. The train seemed to be in the molecules of air.

By the time it had passed, there were only 30 seconds left in the piece. The boat still was not entirely set, so we were working harder than we needed, but we had speed in spite of the check. Our oars dipped into ribbons of sunlight. The river was no longer glass. It was flame.

---

Andrew Carnegie laid the groundwork for Carnegie Tech, which became Carnegie Mellon, in the last years of the 19th century. We studied him that March in Demarest's class. We argued about him across the seminar table, called him a philanthropist, a robber baron, or a ripe bastard. However, I admired his practical idealism. When proposing his idea for a university in a letter to the mayor of Pittsburgh, Carnegie assured the mayor that he was prepared to support the project. "My heart is in the work," he wrote. But just in case, he equipped Baker Hall, where Demarest's class met, with sloping floors that would allow the movement of heavy machinery. That way, should the university fail, the campus could be easily converted into a factory. He knew how to fill space. The school that is now Carnegie Mellon, the classrooms where I studied, began as a trade school. A portion of it was indeed a factory in the early 1900s. Students welded steel and practiced bricklaying in the cavernous space where I later attended lectures and prepared for a life of writing and teaching.

---

My two worst rowing habits were rushing up the slide and catching late. After a couple of speed pieces, exhaustion laid its weight on every muscle, and these habits surfaced. I occupied my space less and less effectively, felt my oar hanging in space before it dropped into the water. My teammates were working without me for a split second every stroke. "I can read the Bible in the time it takes you to catch!" Oliver yelled across the water. He came alongside us and we all began to drive a little harder off our legs. "Catch! Drrriiive!" He used the megaphone to make his voice sound mechanical. "Catch! Driiivveeee!"

Daylight had come in earnest and we were below the shining glass skyscrapers, which were supported by steel, housing technology firms enjoying the dot-com boom. Fresh from the ruins, seeing the world as I did, I wondered what separated technology from industry besides a few decades and a stretch of river.

The bridges were golden and flared pink in the morning sunlight. Everyone in Pittsburgh could see the skyscrapers, the bustle of commerce, the traffic streaming across the bridges. Only rowers were treated daily to a view of what was holding everything up. Steel bolts passing through steel plates, like massive knuckles gripping an arm; long girders where pigeons made their nests. The sunlight came through the railroad bridges and backlit a grid of triangles and rectangles. Form and function. Rowers dream of this at night, seek it in the mornings. It was all around us, like molecules of water. How long until this also would be abandoned?

For a field trip in Demarest's class that April, we rode an incline up Mount Washington, so named because Washington surveyed for Fort Pitt from its brow. The row of businesses and homes that front the peak today are all upscale. These are the restaurants where students go for graduation or to celebrate an anniversary. A luxury apartment building of white concrete and glass catches sunlight. Dr. Demarest told us that the entire hill is riddled with tunnels because they mined Mount Washington for the coal to power the mills upriver. After that day, I'd see the mountain from my boat and imagine those mines could someday reclaim the land above them. The entire mountain might collapse beneath the weight of its own history and crumble into the rivers. Waves would catch our boats like surfboards, and we would balance at the crest of the foaming water, transcending it all.

The final hard piece of the morning was often better than the ones that preceded it. We wanted to leave the river strong. One morning, on the fifth stroke of the power 10, it happened. Not four splashes, or even two, but the single sound of all our blades digging into the water simultaneously. The muffled crack of our oars turning in their locks still echoed in the air when we swung forward and proceeded up the slide uniformly. We did this over and over again until the sound of the oars was joined by another noise that only the bow seat can hear—water flowing rapidly under the hull. It sounds like coffee percolating. The sound, louder to me than all the traffic, meant that we'd achieved run, eliminated all boat check, and accomplished what we set out to do that morning. *Swish, schook, splash. Swish, schook, splash.* Oliver and Laura praised our performance, but we didn't dare say anything. Our voices would have revealed that we were not one body. We were content to be a single voice without speech, sight without eyes. There was only our own industrial chorus, the river speaking to me through the hull, the perfect line of our wake, and, above us, the city of glass and steel.

I often noticed the same man crossing the Sixth Street Bridge in the mornings. At least, I think it was the same man. He looked like a comic book rendition of the middle-aged office worker—balding, a thin brown mustache, carrying a brown briefcase. Sometimes he would look down from the bridge railing, stop, and watch us. He watched us like he was the only one in the city who knew we were there. Perhaps he was. When we rowed downtown, many noticed us, but few saw. Most of the people we passed under every morning still believe that rowers have one oar for each hand, that they sit in one spot and only move their arms and back as they row. They didn't take the time to notice what was true: we had two hands around each thick oar handle and our seats slid forward so we could coil and release our bodies like springs. That's what sight is, I think. It's giving time the opportunity to strip away the layers between belief and truth; it's watching something as if you've never seen it, allowing wonder and energy to wash over you.

I think about the man on the bridge still sometimes. I look back, through the lens of my own post-college life, and believe he was trying to float away with us. I wonder if we were the only beauty he could see. Did he think we looked like water insects? Did he notice that the dark puddles we left in the water healed slowly to silver? And did he see the city itself, its gathering energy, the reflected pink and silver light over us all, the coiled expectation of April's first warm morning? Or was downtown only a canyon of concrete between the parking lot and a cubicle? When we rowed, the ghosts of millworkers made us understand power and pain, but the office workers frightened us. We knew that future awaited us, the end of our luminous journeys through the city. I wondered how much longer I would take the time to see and understand the layers of my surroundings. With each stroke, I focused on driving off the balls of my feet, on pushing the city away. Soon we returned to our section of the river, with its coal trains and abandoned brick warehouses reflecting the sun's fire in their windows. I knew practice was almost over when the ketchup smell from the Heinz factory dominated the air.

**AFTER THE ROW**

It's hard to find people to row with after college ends. I climbed out of a boat the day before graduation five years ago and have not sat in one since. But I have returned to Pittsburgh a handful of times, usually by myself or with some friends who live nearby. They did not row or take Reading the Built Landscape. They like to drive up Mount Washington to look down on the vast expanse of hills, rivers, and skyscrapers. Sometimes we ride the incline. I go along, but then, before I leave town, I drive out to Herr's Island, down the road past the subdivision, the offices and the boathouse. I park at some tennis courts and walk to the upstream tip of the island.

There is a stone staircase leading down to an overlook, lined by stone walls. When the water is low, it's possible to drop over the wall and land on a small spit at river level. From there I can see the roofs of factories upstream, all of them blue or rust-colored. Or I can turn and look downstream, with the skyscrapers and stadiums in the distance, the triangles, arches, and rectangles of bridges stretching to the horizon.

The old Carnegie Steel Works dominates one shore; some of the buildings I remember are gone and some have been converted into offices. I know that entire lives played out there, that I am heading for a similar fate. Along the water, I remember the soaring sensation of achieving run and set, the layers and layers of seeing. The city shimmers and works, and the river surrounds me.

# Acknowledgments

Norman Maclean began the acknowledgments for his lovely and wondrous novella, *A River Runs Through It*, with the following words: *Although it's a little book, it took a lot of help to become a book at all.* Over the years, as I wrote the preceding pages, Maclean's pitch-perfect articulation of his gratitude hummed through my mind. The help I received came from all quarters and went into every aspect of making this book.

My little book would not be a book at all if it were not for the grace and assistance of the folks at Benu Press, who decided that it should be conferred the 2009 Social Justice and Equity in Creative Nonfiction Award. Le Roy and Lesley Chappell have spared no modicum of effort to ensure that I, the author, have a beautiful, polished, and well-promoted memoir. My editor, Sydney James, gently made astute corrections and went through every comma and semi-colon with me.

Before *Confederate Streets* was the book you now hold in your hands, it was a series of Word documents stuffed in a messenger bag between red pens, undergraduate compositions, and textbooks and distributed with varying degrees of hope and trepidation to professors and peers at West Virginia University. I'd wanted to write about busing for years and was finally given that chance in Ethel Morgan Smith's class, Literature of the Civil Rights Movement. Dr. Kevin Oderman was my thesis advisor and responsible for the creative nonfiction workshops at WVU. His constant help throughout this project simply allowed this book to exist. He and his wife, the novelist Sara Pritchard, have continued to provide guidance even though my time as a grad student at WVU ended long ago. The same goes for Dr. John Ernest, whose feedback, scholarly assistance, and expertise in matters pertaining to race and literary theory has been invaluable. Rounding out my thesis committee was Mary Ann Samyn.

Her ability to come in as an outside reader and her sense of the poetic helped me to smooth out the language and gave me a shot of confidence as I prepared to share the manuscript with publishing houses.

My peers at WVU were, frankly, far more helpful and patient than I really deserved, and I certainly appreciated it. Renee Nicholson, Tara Eaton Tensen, Meg Thompson, Sara Einstein, and Jess Queener deserve special mention. We continue to enjoy each other's company and support each other through the successes, failures, and general eccentric occurrences of the writing life.

Part of one chapter of this book, entitled "That's What We're Doing Here," began its life as an essay I wrote for Jane McCafferty's Literary Nonfiction class at Carnegie Mellon University. She was subsequently willing to work with me on an honors thesis the following year, during which time I hashed out, read, experimented on, and most likely butchered the creative nonfiction genre; and her willingness to teach me about a new (to me), beautiful way of seeing and writing was an awakening that set me on my literary path.

If you think about gratitude long enough (an experience I can now heartily recommend), it begins to cut a long, long trail, connecting all sorts of experiences in your life. Being a teacher myself now, I am especially aware of one educational experience flowing into another, so I would be remiss not to mention Bill Brown and G'anne Harmon, the high school English teachers who read my poems as though I were a colleague.

Even with all the publishing fortune and education and wonderful peers in the world, my little book would not be a book if it weren't for research. I'd always imagined research as being a solitary pursuit executed in a study carrel in some lonesome corner of a library, and to an extent it was, but research is also an exhilaratingly connective experience. Dot Butler, Becky Long, Janet Murphy, Sara Smith, and Vanzetta Whittaker all shared their memories of busing and racial politics at Percy Priest Elementary School. Research librarian and Pearl High School alumna Chantay Steptoe, who sadly passed away in 2009, mailed me packets of articles from the library at *The Tennessean*. Other Pearl High alumni who assisted with my research were Rip Patton and Linda T. Wynn. I am also indebted to Ted Lenox and Melvin Black, who took me on a tour of the museum they curate in "Old Pearl." The research staff at Metro-Nashville Public Schools helped me pull together the enrollment statistics I use throughout my essays on education.

The chapter about my church's connections to the Civil Rights

Movement could not have been completed without assistance from long-time member Leon Cunningham, the widow of the minister on whom the essay is focused Helen Dodson, former associate minister Rosemary Brown, current minister Peter Van Eys, and church historian Dave Nichols. And all the research I did on music would have been pretty directionless if it were not for Michael Gray and the good folks at the Country Music Hall of Fame, who allowed me to schedule research time in the museum's stunning top-floor library.

I also owe a debt of gratitude to a number of authors whose books I relied on—the late music historians Charles K. Wolfe and David C. Morton, who rediscovered DeFord Bailey near the end of his life; the late David Halberstam, whose book *The Children* alerted me to the vital history that had played out on streets I thought I knew so well; Dr. Richard Pride, who co-authored *The Burden of Busing* and graciously read through my own essays on that topic. Tim Wise, the antiracism activist who grew up in the same area of Nashville as me and wrote his own experience down in *White Like Me*, has been a huge source of encouragement over the past two years, and I am honored that he reads and respects my work.

A few of the chapters here were previously published in literary journals. I'd like to thank Bret Lott, formerly of *The Southern Review*, Hattie Fletcher of *Creative Nonfiction*, and Richard Matthews of the *Tampa Review* for committing my words to print. I would also like to thank the good people at the Hambidge Center in Rabun Gap, Georgia, for allowing me two glorious weeks to pull this little book together and ready it for publication submissions during the summer of 2009.

As I mentioned earlier, I am now a teacher myself. Although my friends, colleagues, and students at the McCallie School in Chattanooga, Tennessee came into my life relatively late in the process of making this book, I don't think I would have persevered through that final, difficult push without them. My colleagues are wonderful listeners. My students bring insight and new ideas to the table in ways that only teenagers can, and I have learned from them.

A small group of people deserves special recognition for this, my first book. They've been there since I first started carrying a composition book and winning little embossed certificates and twenty-dollar bills in local contests. No decision to pursue writing at any level would have come without the support and encouragement of my longtime best friend, Paula Pfleiger Thrasher; my eternal partner in writing and exuberance, Austin Adkinson; or my core group of lifelong church friends: Kris and Allison

Lott, Brandon Baxter, Elizabeth Griggs Brandau, and Lelia Holscher Eads. The same goes for Eddie, Lynn, and Chris Tucker, who are so dear to me that it defies even Norman Maclean's capacity for articulation.

The influence of my mother, Margaret, my father, Steve, and my sister, Cathleen, imbues every page. If you think a book requires a lot of help to become a book at all, you should see how much work it took to turn me into a person with the capacity to sit still and reflect on anything whatsoever. My parents' willingness to share their interests in writing and history, combined with my sister's intelligent repartee and sweet patience with life in a family of attention-deficited writers and history buffs, lies at the core of who I am. I love them very much, and it is to my mother, father, and sister that I dedicate this little book.

## Source Acknowledgements

The following chapters were previously printed in the following literary journals, to whom I owe a great deal of gratitude. Special thanks goes to Fleda Brown and the rest of the selection committee who chose "Our Most Segregated Hour" as the winner of the 2007 AWP Intro Journals Award for Creative Nonfiction.

"Our Most Segregated Hour." *Tampa Review* 35, (Spring/Summer 2008).
"Rowing Through the Ruins." *Pittsburgh in Words*, spec. issue of Creative Nonfiction (Fall 2008).
"That's What We're Doing Here." *The Southern Review* 42, no. 3, (Summer 2006).

# Partial Bibliography

During most of my research for *Confederate Streets*, I sought to educate myself on the historical context for the circumstances of my own life in the city where I was raised. For this general foundation, I pored over old newspaper articles and interviewed the teachers and other local experts listed in my acknowledgements. For more specific knowledge, I consulted these sources:

## Music

Bain, Rebecca. "Harmonica Great DeFord Bailey Gets His Due." www.npr.org. National Public Radio, 12 Nov. 2005. Web. 19 Nov., 2006.

Havighurst, Craig. *Air Castle of the South: WSM and the Making of Music City*. Urbana: University of Illinois Press, 2007. Print.

Kingsbury, Paul, ed. *The Encyclopedia of Country Music*. New York: Oxford University Press, 1998. Print.

Kyriakoudas, Louis M. "The Grand Ole Opry and the Urban South." *Southern Cultures* 10.1 (2004): 67-84. Print.

Malone, Bill C., and David Stricklin. *Southern Music / American Music*. Lexington: University Press of Kentucky, 2003. Print.

Morton, David, and Charles K. Wolfe. *DeFord Bailey: A Black Star in Early Country Music*. Knoxville: The University of Tennessee Press, 1991. Print.

Rutter, John. Gloria: *Vocal Score*. New York: Oxford University Press, 1976. Print.

Wolfe, Charles K. *A Good-Natured Riot: The Early Years of the Grand Ole Opry*. Nashville: The Country Music Foundation Press and Vanderbilt University Press, 1999. Print.

———. "Rural Black String Music." *Black Music Research Journal* 10.1 (1990): 32-35. Print.

## Race Theory

Du Bois, W.E.B. "Criteria of Negro Art." *African-American Literary Theory*. Ed. Winston Napier. New York: New York University Press, 2000. 17-24. Print.

Mills, Charles. *The Racial Contract*. Ithaca, New York: Cornell University Press, 1997. Print.

Morrison, Toni. *Playing in the Dark: Whiteness and the Literary Imagination*. New York: Vintage Books, 1993. Print.

Wise, Tim. *White Like Me: Reflections on Race from a Privileged Son*. 2nd ed. New York: Soft Skull Press, 2007. Print.

## Civil Rights and Immigration History

Bell, Thomas. *Out of this Furnace: A Novel of Immigrant Labor in America*. 1941. Pittsburgh: University of Pittsburgh Press, 1976.

Bodnar, John, Roger Simon, and Michael P. Weber. *Lives of Their Own: Blacks, Italians, and Poles in Pittsburgh, 1900-1960*. Urbana: University of Illinois Press, 1983. Print.

Halberstam, David. *The Children*. New York: Fawcett Books, 1998. Print.

McWhorter, Diane. *Carry Me Home*. New York: Simon and Schuster, 2002. Print.

Pride, Dana. "The Great Divide." *Nashville: An American Self Portrait*. Ed. John Egerton and E. Thomas Wood. Nashville: Beaten Biscuit Press, 2001. 245-269. Print.

Pride, Richard, and J. David Woodward. *The Burden of Busing: The Politics of Desegregation in Nashville, Tennessee*. Knoxville: The University of Tennessee Press, 1985. Print.

## Miscellaneous

Thomas, Dylan. *A Child's Christmas in Wales*. Cambridge, Mass: Candlewick Press, 2004. (Print)

## About the Author

ERIN E. TOCKNELL was born and raised in Nashville, but has lived and studied in Pittsburgh, Penn., Kalispell, Mont. and Morgantown, W.Va. Once an award-winning staff reporter for the *Columbia Daily Herald* in Columbia, Tenn., her essays have been published in *The Southern Review*, *Creative Nonfiction*, and the *Tampa Review*. In 2007 she was the winner of the AWP Intro Journals Award for creative nonfiction. She currently resides in Chattanooga, Tenn., where she teaches literature and writing and coaches rowing at the The McCallie School.

## About Benu Press

**Benu Press** is a small, independent press committed to publishing poetry, fiction, and creative non-fiction. We believe in the transformative power of literature. To that end, we seek to publish inspiring and thought-provoking books about the practical dimensions of social justice and equity.

Also published by Benu Press:

*March on Milwaukee: A Memoir of the Open Housing Protests* (script), Margaret Rozga
*Language is Power*, Stephanie Reid
*Confederate Streets*, Erin Tocknell
*Though I Haven't Been to Baghdad*, Margaret Rozga (Spring 2011)
*Love Rise Up*, edited by Steve Fellner and Phil Young
*High Notes*, Lois Roma-Deeley
*Two Hundred Nights and One Day*, Margaret Rozga
*All Screwed Up*, Steve Fellner

For more information: http://www.benupress.com